ISBN 978-1-332-00248-1
PIBN 10266489

1 MONTH OF
FREE
READING

at

www.ForgottenBooks.com

By purchasing this book you are eligible for one month membership to ForgottenBooks.com, giving you unlimited access to our entire collection of over 700,000 titles via our web site and mobile apps.

To claim your free month visit: www.forgottenbooks.com/free266489

English
Français
Deutsche
Italiano
Español
Português

www.forgottenbooks.com

Mythology Photography **Fiction**
Fishing Christianity **Art** Cooking
Essays Buddhism Freemasonry
Medicine **Biology** Music **Ancient**
Egypt Evolution Carpentry Physics
Dance Geology **Mathematics** Fitness
Shakespeare **Folklore** Yoga Marketing
Confidence Immortality Biographies
Poetry **Psychology** Witchcraft
Electronics Chemistry History **Law**
Accounting **Philosophy** Anthropology
Alchemy Drama Quantum Mechanics
Atheism Sexual Health **Ancient History**
Entrepreneurship Languages Sport
Paleontology Needlework Islam
Metaphysics Investment Archaeology
Parenting Statistics Criminology
Motivational

THE BEEF BONANZA;

OR,

HOW TO GET RICH ON THE PLAINS.

BEING A DESCRIPTION OF

CATTLE-GROWING, SHEEP-FARMING, HORSE-RAISING, AND DAIRYING

IN THE WEST.

BY

GEN. JAMES S. BRISBIN, U.S.A.,

AUTHOR OF "BELDEN, THE WHITE CHIEF," "LIFE OF GENERAL GRANT,"
"LIFE OF J. A. GARFIELD," "LIFE OF GEN. W. S. HANCOCK."

WITH ILLUSTRATIONS.

PHILADELPHIA:

J. B. LIPPINCOTT & CO.

LONDON: 16 SOUTHAMPTON ST., COVENT GARDEN.

1881.

CHAPTER V.

MILLIONS IN BEEF.

CHAPTER VI.

GREAT LANDS IN THE SOUTHWEST.

CHAPTER VII.

MORE ABOUT CATTLE-LANDS.

SHEEP-FARMING IN THE WEST.

CHAPTER VIII.

GREAT OPPORTUNITIES.

CHAPTER IX.

GREAT PASTURE-LANDS.

CHAPTER X.

A SHEEP-RANCH.

HORSE-RAISING IN THE WEST.

CHAPTER XI.

HORSE-RAISING IN THE WEST.

DAIRYING OUT WEST.

CHAPTER XII.

THE GIFT OF THE COWS.

STOCK-GROWING OUT WEST.

CHAPTER XIII.

MONTANA.

APPENDIX.

LIST OF ILLUSTRATIONS.

INTRODUCTORY.

On the atlases of thirty or forty years ago, when the stock of information concerning the territory now comprised in the flourishing States of Kansas and Nebraska, and in Eastern Colorado and Dakota, was exceedingly limited, the whole of it was represented as the " Great American Desert." The boy who studied geography then conceived an affection for this desert, a fact which did honor to his patriotism. His country had the highest mountains, the greatest lakes, and the largest rivers in the world, and it flattered his national pride to see on its map a desert which rivalled in size anything the Old World could produce in the same line. There was one natural feature of the Eastern Continent which humbled his pride of country somewhat. This was the terrible Maelstrom on the coast of Norway, that furious whirlpool which the Western World had nothing to match. But he has lived to see that unmatched whirlpool robbed of its terrors. It is almost surveyed out of existence, and in its present condition it does not greatly outrank the late Hell Gate in New York harbor. With the disappearance of the hated Maelstrom, however, he has had the mortification to see his favorite desert vanish from the map. That barren terra-incognita of his youth is now one of the finest grazing regions on the globe, and a large portion of it is yielding excellent crops to the agriculturist. This ancient desert has been for a long time the favorite pasturing ground of the buffalo, and it doubtless now contains more domestic cattle than it ever did buffaloes.

The eastern boundary of the old desert was the Missouri River, and it is fresh in the memory of many that when settlement began on the west bank of that river it was supposed its natural limit would be in the immediate vicinity of the stream. Gradually the desert was pushed westward a hundred miles, as far as the Big Blue, which was fixed upon as its eastern boundary. But the farmers did not stop here. They continued to plough up the eastern edge of the desert until it was moved another hundred miles west, to Fort Kearney, where it was supposed it would forever remain. This frontier was about in the middle of the desert as originally laid out by Lewis and Clark, and it was thought that here at least the spirit of innovation would be satisfied. Nevertheless, the farmers continued to push westward, and now the occupants of the remaining portion of the great waste are viewing with alarm the persistent demonstration of the fertility of their desert domain. The great cattle-kings claim that the country is utterly unfit for cultivation, to which the farmers reply by ploughing up a strip on its eastern edge every year some ten miles wide, and raising good crops.

The cattle-kings fear the utter destruction of their fine ranges in prospect unless something can be done to establish their desert character. They need have no cause for alarm. There is an American Desert in the far West which can never be used for any other purpose than the raising of great herds. It is of these lands and the cattle upon them the following pages treat.

The plains of the West, instead of being barren and worthless as early geographers supposed, have become one of the richest parts of our public domain. The vast beef reservoir they contain is now the fit subject of an interesting volume.

PREFACE.

THE NEW WEST.

I HAVE been a resident of the West for twelve years, and my official duties have called me during that time into nearly every State and Territory between the Missouri and the Pacific Coast. Almost every valley, hill, mountain, and pass of which I have written has been ridden over by me on horseback, and I have observed everywhere the unbounded capacity of the West, not only for stock-growing, but farming, mining, and manufacturing. To me the West is a never-ceasing source of wonder, and I cannot imagine why people remain in the over-crowded East, while so many lands and chances are to the west of them. The West to-day is not what it was yesterday, and it will not be to-morrow what it is to-day. New discoveries, new developments and improvements are constantly being made, and a new West springing up.

The West! The mighty West! That land where the buffalo still roams and the wild savage dwells; where the broad rivers flow and the boundless prairie stretches away for thousands of miles; where new States are every year carved out and myriads of people find homes and wealth; where the poor professional young man, flying from the over-crowded East and the tyranny of a moneyed aristocracy, finds honor and wealth; where the young politician, unoppressed by rings and combinations, relying upon his own abilities, may rise to position and fame; where there are lands for the landless, money for the moneyless, briefs for lawyers, patients for doctors, and above all, labor and its reward for every poor man who is willing to work. This is the West as I have known it for twelve years, and learned to love it because of its grateful return to all those who have tried to improve it. Its big-hearted people never push a young man back, but generously help him on, and so, by being great themselves, have learned how to make others great. "Where had I best settle?" "Where can I buy the cheapest and best land?" "Where will I be safe?" "Where can I raise the best stock?" These are questions asked every day by people all over the East. In vain do they look into books and newspapers for answers to their inquiries; they are not to be found; at least, not truthful ones. I do not suppose I can supply all the information required, but I can give my impressions, which shall at least have the merit of being honest. I believe Kansas and Iowa are the best unsettled farming States; Nebraska is the best State for farming and stock-raising combined; Colorado is the best State for sheep-growing, farming, and mining; Wyoming is the best Territory for cattle-growing alone; Montana is the best Territory for cattle-growing and mining.

It does not matter where the emigrant settles in the

West, so he comes; and he will almost anywhere soon find himself better off than if he had remained East.

When I visit the Eastern States, it is a matter of astonishment to me to learn how little is known of the advantages, resources, and interests of the West. The masses do not seem to understand what is west of them, and cling to the hilly, stony, and unproductive lands where they were raised rather than move to an unknown country. Often I hear city young men in the East say, " If I had only come here twenty years ago, I might now be a rich man. Land then sold for a few dollars a foot, while now it is worth as many hundreds or even thousands." So, too, the young farmer exclaims, "Land is so high, I can never afford to buy a farm. When my father settled here and bought, it was worth only $10, $20, or $30 per acre, and now it is held at $100, and were I to buy a farm, and pay the purchase-money down, I could not more than raise the interest on the balance; therefore, I can never hope to own a farm of my own." Every one East seems to think the days for speculation are over, and they regret a hundred times a year they had not been born fifty years sooner. To the discouraged let me say, be of good heart and come West, for what has been occurring in the East during the last two hundred years is now occurring in the West, only with tenfold more rapidity. Young men, when your fathers bought the homes and land which they now own, and on which you were raised, there were no railroads, and emigration was necessarily slow. Their property has been thirty, forty, or even fifty years in reaching its

present value. Not so the West. Railroads are everywhere, and ten or twenty years at most will do for
you what it took your fathers fifty years to accomplish.
Millions of people are pressing westward, and settle
where you may you will soon find yourself surrounded by neighbors, not in twos and threes as were
your fathers, but by hundreds and thousands of new-
comers. The growth of this West of ours has been
the miracle of the nineteenth century, and its improve-
ment has as yet only fairly begun. The Old World
annually pours myriads of people upon our Western
shores, and to these we add hundreds of thousands
from our native population, who find new homes each
year. The increase and development of the West is,
therefore, not to be wondered at, for it has the best
facilities of any land in the world. In one year 390,000
foreign emigrants landed in the United States, and
these did not include 30,000 Chinese and 2000 Cana-
dians. When the emigration from foreign sources,
which has been interrupted by domestic war, shall have
been restored to its natural flow, the influx will probably reach the following figures: Landing at New York,
350,000; at San Francisco, 100,000; at Philadelphia,
50,000; at Portland, Oregon, 10,000; at New Orleans,
10,000; at Galveston, Texas, 10,000; total, 530,000.
Of these fully 300,000 will come West, and the re-
mainder scatter through the South and East. Add to
the Western emigration 200,000 from native sources,
and we shall have half a million people annually seek-
ing homes in the West. It will not be very long until
the annual accessions to our population will equal the

whole number of inhabitants living in the United States at the time they achieved their independence from Great Britain. The course of Prussia toward the German States, in consolidating them into an empire, and creating an emperor by dethroning kings who were the legitimate rulers of their people, and in appointing over these people distasteful governors, has caused thousands of wealthy Germans to seek our shores, and will cause many thousands more to come. When a people lose their country they do not often care for their homes, and the Germans feel that they are no longer Germans, but Prussians, who would prefer rather to be Americans. The Chinese, after being walled in for two thousand years, have at last found a place to emigrate to, and, unless prevented, millions of them will eventually come to the United States. The sympathy ever manifested by our people for Ireland's starving millions will reinvigorate emigration from that unhappy country to our shores. The result of all this will be to settle up the West and double our population, large as it is. Young men who have polled their first vote will live to see the day when the United States will contain 100,000,000 of people. What must be apparent to every one, and what ought to be impressed on the minds of men, both old and young, is the fact that there will soon be no unsettled West. Several lines of emigration have already penetrated across the continent, and settlements are rapidly spreading from the right and left of them until they intersect each other, and when the West is settled, what then? Then, indeed, will the young men have cause to say, "If we had only been born thirty years sooner we might have become rich." There will then be no unoccupied lands; no homestead laws; no West to seek. The country, one vast sea of cities, towns, villas, and farms, will stretch out from ocean to ocean, and in America, as in England, the highest claim to wealth and respectability will be the proprietorship of the soil. Do you ask who will live to see the country settled? I answer, thousands of men and women who are now in middle life; and even old men may yet live to see the day when those rich prairie lands of ours, now to be had by living upon them, will bring $50 per acre. The veteran grandfather who will come West can live long enough to see towns and cities spring up, and farms dot the land all over where now only the wild Indian and the buffalo are found. Why stick to the rocky and unproductive hill-sides of the East, when the best, rich, level prairie lands and beautiful homes can be had for $10 per acre? Or, if the emigrant is too poor to buy, he can take up one, two, three, or four hundred acres, and if he will but live on them for five years, they are his and his children's after him forever. A great deal of sport a few years ago was made of Horace Greeley for so often repeating his advice, "Go West, young man; go West and take a farm, and grow up with the country." But after living in the West twelve years, I can safely say that never did any man give better advice to the youth of a nation. No industrious man can make a mistake in moving West, and if I had a son to advise, I should by all means say to him, "Go West as soon as you can; get a good piece of land, and hold on to it." Of the subjects concerning which I shall write in the following volume, I can only say they do not by any means embrace the best interests of the West, large and lucrative as they are in themselves. Farming may be set down first, mining second, stock-growing third, and manufacturing fourth among the great advantages of the West. Of these subjects only one—stock-growing—will be written upon by me, and it is my hope some abler pen will write up the other great resources and interests of the mighty and unknown Far West.

JAMES S. BRISBIN,
U. S. Army.

CATTLE-GROWING OUT WEST.

CATTLE-GROWING OUT WEST.

CHAPTER I.

THE LAND TO THE WEST OF US.

The Great Grazing-Lands of the Plains—Increase of Population
and Decrease of Cattle—Cattle-Kings of Nebraska and
Wyoming—The Herds and Where they Graze.

THE increasing interest felt among all classes of
people East regarding stock-growing in the West and
the profits to be derived from this occupation induces
me to offer the public information gathered at various
times during a residence of twelve years on the Plains
among the herds.

Let me premise by saying that in the whole world
there are but five great natural grazing-grounds, located
in Central Asia, South Africa, South America, Australia, and on the plains of America. The first is larger
in extent than all Europe; the second is as great; the
third half as much; the fourth as large as South
America; and the fifth, the boundless plains of the
United States, contain 1,650,000 square miles with
over a billion of acres.

These pastoral lands of ours have never been under-

stood or appreciated. The day will come when the
government will derive more taxes from the grazing
country than the best agricultural regions. These arid
plains, so long considered worthless, are the natural
meat-producing lands of the nation, and in a few years
30,000,000 of people will draw their beef from them.
All the figures I have seen published have rather
understated than overestimated their capacity.

In 1869 the whole of the live-stock in the United
States was estimated to be worth $1,500,000,000. In
1840 the average number of cattle in America to every
100 persons was less than 100 head, and in 1850
only about 75 head to 100 people. In 1860 the
States and Territories had the following ratio to 100
people: Alabama, 81 head; Arkansas, 126; California, 387; Connecticut, 48; Delaware, 51; Florida,
274; Georgia, 95; Illinois, 87; Indiana, 87; Iowa,
79; Kansas, 81; Kentucky, 72; Louisiana, 73;
Maine, 59; Maryland, 37; Massachusetts, 22; Michigan, 71; Minnesota, 68; Mississippi, 91; Missouri,
98; New Hampshire, 81; New Jersey, 34; New
York, 50; North Carolina, 69; Ohio, 70; Oregon,
292; Pennsylvania, 48; Rhode Island, 22; South
Carolina, 72; Tennessee, 68; Texas, 579; Vermont,
115; Virginia, 65; Wisconsin, 66; District of Columbia, 1; Dakota, 30; Nebraska, 100; New Mexico,
108; Utah, 100; Washington Territory, 259. The
stock-producing region of Wyoming was then unknown.
If we consult the tables it will be observed that if
cattle-breeding in the United States was stopped for
five years all the cattle would be eaten up. Since 1860

four States and Territories have increased their stock, five have stood still, and thirty have decreased in comparison with the population. The rapid increase of our population will soon require that more cattle be raised, or we shall have to pay higher prices for beef. The number of people is increasing much faster than the number of cattle. The receipts of cattle in Chicago in 1867 were 334,188, as against 324,599 in 1868, showing a decrease in one year of 9659 head brought to market. Since then the cattle product of Wyoming has done something to relieve the Chicago market, but the number has not kept pace with the increase of population in that city. In 1863 cattle brought in Chicago $4.80 per hundred; in 1864, $7.52; in 1865, $8.46; in 1866, $7.72; in 1867, $8.02; and in 1868, $8.10. In 1867 the value of meat consumed in the United States was $1,396,643,699, and in 1868, $1,337,111,-822, showing that notwithstanding the increased value of stock there was a decrease in the total value of $59,531,877. Since then we have no accurate reports, but the ratio of annual increase of stock in the country is about $1\frac{3}{4}$ per cent. So we must raise more cattle, or in a few years pay higher prices for beef. This view of the case is most encouraging to the stock-growers, and shows conclusively the importance of the cattle trade. For ten years at least yet the stock-growers need have no fear of overstocking the beef market.

As before stated, the great pasture-lands of the country aggregate over one million square miles, and are located principally along the Rio Grande, Ncuces, San Antonio, Guadalupe, Colorado, Brazos, Trinity,

Main Red, Washita, Canadian, Cimaron, Arkansas, Smoky Hill, Saline, Salmon Fork, Republican, North and South Plattes, Loup Fork, Niobrara, White Earth, Big Cheyenne, Little Missouri, Powder River, Tongue, Rosebud, Big Horn, Wind Rivers, Yellowstone, Milk River, Musselshell, Marias, Jefferson, and Missouri. The length of these streams is over twenty thousand miles. The small streams on the eastern slope of the Rocky Mountains are the Blue Water, Cold Water, Hill Creek, Raw Hide, Muddy Willow, Shawnee, Slate, Sweet Water, Ash, Pumpkin, Laramie, Carter, Cottonwood, Horseshoe, Elkhorn, Deer Creek, Medicine Bow, Rock Creek, Douglas, Lodge Pole, Big Laramie, Little Laramie, and north-south forks of Platte, Horse Creek, Beaver, Pawnee, Crow, Lone Tree, Big Beaver, Bijou, Kiowa, and Bear Creeks, and Cache-la-Poudre. The Plattes are the best grazing-grounds east of Montana, and the Cache-la-Poudre and Big Thompson rank next. The grazing-lands on these two streams alone are put as high as 12,000,000 acres. The Cache-la-Poudre is famous for its fine vegetables as well as its grazing. I have myself seen cabbage-heads raised there that weighed fifty pounds each, turnips twelve pounds, and potatoes three pounds. The climate in the grazing-country I have described is fine, the temperature in summer averaging from 45 to 75 and 90 degrees, and in winter 30 to 32 degrees. The mean temperature for the year is 50 to 55 degrees. Out of the 365 days in the year 275 are clear. The snow-line in the east, on the White Mountains, is fixed at an elevation of 7000 feet; on the Alleghanies at 7200; and on the Rocky

Mountains at 12,000. Vegetation ceases on the White Mountains at 5000, on the Alleghanies at 5500, while in the Black Hills of the West, at Sherman, at 8200 feet high vegetation is rank. Strawberries grow on the tops of the mountains, and evergreen-trees flourish at an elevation of 11,000 feet. There is little difference between the climate of the Plains and the Atlantic Coast. The rainfall on the Plains has greatly increased of late years, and the average is eighteen inches per annum, divided as follows: spring, $8\frac{69}{100}$; summer, $5\frac{70}{100}$; autumn, $3\frac{90}{100}$ inches. The snowfall is also about eighteen inches. Later in this volume I shall present a theory for the prevailing high winds on the Plains, and also give letters from Sir Roderick Murchison and several army officers relative to the cause of the mildness of the climate in such a high latitude, but I have said enough about the climate for the present, and sufficient, I think, to convince any one that the Great American Desert is not such a bad place to live, and indeed no desert at all.

CHAPTER II.

GREAT LANDS AND GREAT OWNERS.

Ranches along the Platte River—Herds in Wyoming and Nebraska—Their Increase and Profits—Cattle-Kings—The Great Stock-Drivers, who they are and how they Operate.

I VISITED the herds of the Plattes and made careful inquiry as to the number of cattle, names of owners, and profits to be derived from cattle-breeding.

On the Laramie Plains I saw the finest cattle, and one herd in particular pleased me, a drove of 1500 cows, with 2300 calves of various ages. First we came upon a few stragglers, or warders, guarding the herd, who seemed to be sentinels over the calves. Next we found families of two, four, and six, in groups, then bunches of a dozen, and lastly the great body of the herd. The cows were Texas, bred to large Durham bulls, and the calves bore strongly the impress of the male. Nearly all had thick necks, sturdy bodies, and seemed very healthy. I saw one enormous bull, and near him a cow with three calves, one a two-year-old, one a yearling, and one about two weeks old. It was a grand sight, this herd of 1500 cows, 50 bulls, and 2300 calves. They were much scattered, covering the prairie for miles, and seemed an endless mass of beef for one man to possess; yet I was told that the gentleman who

28

A VIEW FROM SAFE QUARTERS.

A VIEW FROM SAFE QUARTERS.

H.M.SNIDER

owned this herd had three larger ones. I saw a little calf just taking his first steps on the prairie, and stopped to observe him. The cow ran away at my approach, but immediately came back and stood resolutely and defiantly by her young; indeed, so wicked did she look, that the driver whipped up his horses and got away as soon as possible. These Texas cows are dangerous if approached too closely, and, from the fire in the beast's eyes, I am sure she was going to charge.

It is a study to observe the habits of the prairie cattle. They run in families like buffalo, the cows keeping their calves with them sometimes until they are three or four years old. It frequently happens that the mother has under her protection sons and daughters larger than herself. The cow watches over her offspring, and when they disobey punishes them with her horns, to which they tamely submit, like well-trained children. In the middle of the day the cattle leave the high grounds and go to the river bottoms for water, and about nightfall return to the high grounds. In travelling back and forth to the water they march in single file, using the same paths as the buffalo, and, like them, wear deep ruts in the earth. The cattle frequently go four and five miles to water, but, having slaked their thirst, nearly always return to the same ground from which they started out. The following are the names of some of the principal cattle-owners in Wyoming Territory and Western Nebraska. In Lincoln County, Western Nebraska, near North Platte, a station on the Union Pacific Railroad, the following owners keep the number of cattle set opposite their names:

Reith & Barton	6500
Coe, Carter & Pratt	4000
Bent & Evans	2000
Russell & Watt	1800
Webster & Randall	1000
D. W. Baker	500
Major Walker	400
George W. Plummer	1000
S. P. Lang	500
Arnold & Richie	900
Ed. Welch	650
George Burke	500
Charles McDonald	200
Blake & Lyford	300
Jack McCullough	175
J. E. Evans	70

In the vicinity of Ogallala, Nebraska, another station on the Union Pacific Railroad, the following herds graze:

Lonergan Brothers	400
James Boyd	2,500
Paxton & Sharp	6,000
Bosler & Irving	4,000
Bosler & Lawrence	2,500
J. H. Bosler	10,000
Searle Brothers	550
L. M. Stone	80
Bradley, Ten Broeck & Co.	1,000
Sheidley Brothers	1,800
George Green	200
Wild Pete	175
G. W. Barnhart	50
Walrath Brothers	600
John Lute	250
Millet & Maybray	4,000
Pratt & Ferris	2,500

On the Republican River, about seventy miles south of Ogallala, there are a number of small herds and one or two large ones. The following are the names of some of the owners:

Bolles & Doyle	300
J. H. Jones	400
Beauvals	275
Mr. Ross	1300

Near Julesburg, Union Pacific Railroad, the owners are:

Edward Meagee	175
Captain Coffman	1900
Keline & Son	2500
C. McCarty	125
James Wear	70
Harkinson & Griffin	500
Broughton & Tassal	3000
Grady Brothers (cows)	60
Wheeler & Merchant	1200
Tusler Brothers	1800
Charles A. Moore	2000
D. B. Lynch	450
R. C. Howard	560
Tom Kane	1000
Harry Newman	550
Callahan & Musherd	200
John Coad & Brother	3000
Adams, Reddington & Co.	2000
Foley & Center	150
Frank Wright	110
J. D. May	120
Hungate & Co.	70
Mr. Borgynist (cows)	60

The great headquarters of the cattle-men of Wyoming Territory is Cheyenne. The herds are scattered over a wide extent of land. Here are the names of the principal owners:

Stout & Stewart, Horse Creek	100
A. M. Rogers, Crow Creek	120
A. H. Reel, Pole Creek	360
W. Rowlands, Muddy Creek	80
W. W. Sawyer, Clingwater Creek	270
D. S. Shaw, Horse Creek	350
R. G. Strause, Richard Creek	160
J. Phillips, Clingwater Creek	150
J. Leoniwan, Sibil Creek	250
F. M. Phillips, Clingwater Creek	1400
Lomis & Trimble, Horse Creek	900
H. N. Orr & Co., Horse Creek	700
David Lannen, Pole Creek	350
Maynard & Co., Horse Creek	1500
B. A. Sheidly, Horseshoe Creek	3000
F. Schwartz, Pole Creek	150
Swan Brothers, Sibil Creek	1800
Snyder & Wolfgen, Sibil Creek	1500
George A. Searight, Horse Creek	1200
Sturgis & Goodell, Fir Creek	1500
D. Trevitt, Cheyenne Creek	140
C. H. Terry, Lone Tree Creek	130
D. C. Tracy, Pine Bluff Creek	1400
W. H Wirkman, Horse Creek	180
J. M. Wooliver, Bear Creek	300
R. Whalen, Clingwater Creek	280
Jack Abney, Crow Creek	60
Alfred Bishop, Crow Creek	100
J. Arthur, Bitter Cottonwood Creek	500
M. A. Arnold, Crow Creek	1400
John Boyd, Richard Creek	210
C. Culver, Horse Creek	1000
B. B. Bishop, Crow Creek	130

W. R. Blove, *Bear* Creek 400
Creighton & Co., Horse Creek 6000
C. E. Clay, Clingwater Creek 150
M. V. *Boughton, Bear* Creek 1800
Colonel *Bullock, Bear* Creek 1000
Harvey Clayton, Horse Creek 200
Kent & Gueterman, Sibil Creek 1000
D. H. Russell, Sibil Creek. 200
R. Layton, Horse Creek 110
D. J. Lykins, Horse Creek 400
McFarland & Co., Clingwater Creek . . . 450
Linderman & Co., Crow Creek 300
F. J. McMahon, Horse Creek 90
J. M. Carey & *Brother*, Crow Creek 6000
H. *B.* Kelly, Clingwater Creek 1800
L. Davis, Horse Creek 180
M. F. Jones, Sibil Creek 900
William Dolan, Muddy Creek 110
H. Jackson, Horse Creek 100
J. A. Dial, Crow Creek 60
A. W. Haygood, Crow Creek 150
Mrs. F. C. Dixon, Pole Creek 70
E. Harkness, Pole Creek 120
Durbin *Brothers*, Horse Creek 1800
Hunter & Abbott, Clingwater Creek. 320
Dawdell & King, Pole Creek 350
O. P. Goodwin, *Bear* Creek 100
Daniel Fallen, Muddy Creek 60
L. George, Richard Creek 250
M. Tagin, Horse Creek 150
J. Freil & *Brother*, Horse Creek 100
J. W. Iliff (deceased), Crow Creek 7000
Webb & Coffey, Horse Creek 1100
E. W. Whitcomb, Crow Creek 1000
Mrs. E. E. Whitney, Horse Creek 60
Thomas Hall, Laramie River 200
Ecoffey & Cuney, Laramie River 1800

There are many other small herds of 50, 100, and

200 head, but these will suffice to show the great cattle business that has grown up on the Plains within the past few years. The oldest of these herds has not been breeding fifteen years. J. W. Iliff, now dead, Joseph M. Carey, J. H. Bosler, and John Creighton have been recognized as the great cattle-kings of the Plains. These men count their herds by the thousands, and will soon count them by tens of thousands.

CHAPTER III.

Profits of Cattle-Raising in Nebraska—Manner of Managing
Herds—Some Notable Ranches and the Profits.

In the last chapter I informed you who the great
cattle-owners of the Northwest were, and in the present
one I shall try to show the increase of their herds and
the profits they are supposed to derive out of their business. Mr. R. C. Keith, of North Platte, began raising
cattle in the fall of 1867, with 5 American cows. The
next year he bought 200 American cows, and in 1869
put in 1000 two- to six-year-old Texas cows. In 1870
he was joined by a partner, and they put in that year
on their ranch 1000 more Texas cattle. In 1872 they
bought 720 Texas steers, cows, two-year-olds, and yearlings ; and also put in later another lot of 250. In
1873 they bought 35 American and 200 Texas cattle.
The total cost of cattle from 1867 to 1873, inclusive,
was under $50,000. This did not include expenses of
ranch, herding, etc., which, however, were small, as they
had no land or timber to buy. They were fortunate in
having old railroad-ties for the hauling, and their ranch
did not cost when finished over $1000, which otherwise
would have cost them fully $2000. They had several
employés. Their men cost $50 per month and board.

They used their men for other purposes as well as herding. They employed one man with the first 1000 head, and got an extra man with the second 1000 head. They were obliged to have two men, as one would not stay at the ranch alone. Mr. Keith could not give any very close figures, as his partner kept the books, but the account of the ranch stood nearly as follows:

Cost of cattle and ranches from 1867 to 1875, inclusive	$55,000
Sold on hoof, 1000 head, mostly cows, which brought, net	33,000
Butchered, 1000 head, which brought	30,000
Total	$63,000
Deduct actual cost of cattle	51,000
Balance	$12,000

Cattle Remaining on Hand.

1400 improved calves, worth $12 each	$16,800
1200 yearlings, worth $18 each	21,600
800 two-year-olds, @ $25 each	20,000
300 three-year-olds, @ $30 each	9,000
200 bulls, @ $50 each	10,000
1300 cows, @ $25 each	32,500
Total value of stock on hand	$109,900

These figures I can indorse as substantially correct, except the value put upon old cows, which I think is a little excessive. Mr. Keith keeps now only one herdsman. This man, when questioned aside from Mr. Keith, said it would be perfectly fair to put the value of the whole herd—old, young, good, bad, and indifferent—on the ranch at $18 per head, or $93,000 for the lot; and he thought they would bring that figure if sold in open market. Making every allowance for exaggerations and mistakes, evidently Mr. Keith's cattle operations have been enormously profitable to him.

The next establishment examined was a combined dairy- and stock-farm, near the Union Pacific Railroad, in Wyoming Territory. The returns showed as follows :

1871.

April, 1871, bought 50 dairy cows, @ $50 each		$2500
" " " 2 bulls		500
Expended on ranch and improvements		1500
Total capital invested		$4500
Expenses of labor	$1500	
Return of butter and milk sold		$1500
47 calves sold		500
Total		$2000
Deduct labor		1500
Profit, 11 per cent.		$500

1872.

Original capital brought down		$4500
Bought 30 cows, @ $50 each		1500
Bought 320 acres of land		800
Expended on improvements		1000
Total capital		$7800
Expenses of labor	$1000	
Returns of butter and milk sold		$2500
Increased value of 47 yearlings		500
62 calves		500
Total		$3500
Deduct labor		1000
Profit, 33⅓ per cent.		$2500

In 1872, 35 mares, at $45 each, 34 mixed cattle, and some furniture were added to the ranch. For the purpose of forming a partnership it was then valued at $15,000, and stood as follows :

October, 1872, dairy ranch as above . . .	$15,000.00
" " bought a herd of mixed cattle, at average prices, comprising 242 yearlings, 336 two-year-olds, 294 three-year-olds, 537 beeves, 379 cows, and 16 horses, at	27,381.94
April, 1873, bought two ranches	950.00
Improvements made in the year	2,410.31
Total capital	$45,742.25
Labor and expenses	$7,200.00
Less portion of labor expended on improvements .	1,900.00
	$5,300.00
Returns of beef and beef cattle	$10,834 65
Returns of butter	2,424.82
Returns of milk	217.43
Returns of sundries, hides, etc.	423.39
Total receipts	$13,900.29
Deduct expenses	5,300.00
Profits	$8,600.29

The total stock remaining on hand was valued at $47,054.86, from which should be deducted $45,742.25, and we have left to profit account . $1,312.61
Add as before stated 8,600.29

Total profit, 21 per cent.	$9,912.90

The estimate of profit in this case is, if anything, rather too low, but shows most satisfactory results.

Thomas Lonergan lives at Ogallala, on the line of

the Union Pacific Railroad, and about 342 miles west from Omaha. He is a cattle-driver, and thoroughly understands his business. His practical experience in cattle, especially of the Texas breeds, is as follows:

1000 head three-year-old bullocks, @ $8.50 each . .	$8,500
1000 " two-year-old " @ $6 " . .	6,000
1000 " yearlings, @ $3.25 each	3,250
1000 " cows, @ $7.50 each	7,500
Expenses 25 horses bought in Texas and used for herding, @ $40 each	1,000
First cost of 100 horses bought in Texas and resold .	4,000
Wages of two foremen, at $150 per month each, four months	1,200
Wages of 26 drivers, with food, $170 per month each, four months	4,420
Eight months' herding on the range, with extra expenses for branding, etc., at the rate of $1 per head per year .	3,334
50 bulls, fair to very fine grades, costing on an average $50 each	2,500
Interest @ 10 per cent., for one year, $41,704 . .	4,170
Total expenses on herd of 4050 head . .	$45,874
Returns, 100 horses sold @ $30 each, a loss of 25 per cent.	$3,000
Amount of investment at end of one year . . .	42,874
Herding six months, from April 1 to October 1 . .	2,500
Interest, half-year @ 10 per cent.	2,143
Total	$50,517
October 1, six months after investment, net returns for sale of 2000 beeves, at an average of $20 each . .	40,000
Net capital account	$10,517

Stock inventory in October, six months after investment, and after sales were completed: 1000 old cows, 500 three-year-olds past, 200 two-year-olds, 1350 calves, 50 bulls, 300 two-year-old heifers; total cattle, 3400 head; horses, saddles, wagons, etc., sufficient for use,

October 1, 1872, six months after investment; capital
account brought down $10,517
October 1, 1873, expenses for one year 5,000
    "   " one year's interest, at 10 per cent. . 1,251

      Total $16,768

October 1, 1873, sales account, 500 bullocks, four-year-
olds, at $25 each, $12,500; October 1, 1873, 100 old
cows, $22.50 each, $2250 . . . . . . $14,750

Balance in capital account, October, 1875, inventory
three and a half years from date of purchase of herd of
5000 head :
1800 old cows, valued at $15 each $27,000
Graded stock, 400 two-year-olds, valued at $12.50 each . 5,000
    275 two-year-old heifers 3,300
    675 " " bullocks 8,300
    75 bulls, @ $50 each 3,750
    1500 yearlings, @ $8 each 12,000
    1850 calves (lot) 9,000

      Total $68,350
Add as profits above outstanding capital account . . 982

Balance to profit, exclusive of 10 per cent. interest . $69,332

The only fault that can be found with this statement
is the price put upon old cows. Mr. Lonergan might
sell them at $22.50 each once or twice, when the de-
mand was great, but I think $17 would be quite suffi-
cient as an average per head upon this kind of stock.
Mr. Lonergan's estimate, however, may be relied upon
as substantially correct, and from it we learn that on an
investment of $60,000 in the course of three and a half
years the capitalist withdraws all but $4000 of his
original capital, receiving in the mean time 10 per cent.
interest, and at the end of the above time finds his stock,

exclusive of horses, wagons, saddles, fixtures, etc., worth $68,359. This is doing an admirable business, and is very encouraging to those who think of investing their money in cattle; but to succeed like Mr. Lonergan one must have patience, shrewdness, and self-reliance, with any amount of energy and capacity, and above all good luck. An Indian raid, a storm, sickness, cattle-disease, or a dozen of unforeseen accidents may arise, whereby all the profits may be cut off, and the capital destroyed. If all goes well there are large profits in driving cattle as well as raising them; but it is rarely all goes well for a year, and while a few make a great deal of money, many make very little, and some lose. To succeed well one must understand the markets, know when to buy and when to sell. Driving is distinct from raising, and it is rarely we find a great driver also an extensive stock-raiser. It may be interesting to know who are the principal drivers as well as stock-raisers in the North-west. The yearly drive is about as follows:

J. Hilsen	7000
J. Chisholm	6000
F. Turksley	1500
Mr. McKidrick	1000
S. Jones	2000
J. B. Martuns	1500
C. C. Cooper	2000
A. W. and U. Black	1500
J. Hart	1000
W. Wilson	800
J. B. Henderson	1600
W. Forsyth	1500
C. C. Campbell	3000
H. Martin	1000
R. Wyte	1500

S. Goldston	1500
J. Anderson	1500
Anderson & Little	1500
J. Patterson	8000
Judge Cary	3000
C. F. Reynolds	5500
C. Goodwight	5000
M. Cavin	1200

There are many smaller drivers, whose names are not given, but the above are the principal movers of stock. Most of the cattle are driven from Texas, but every year the drives will become smaller, as the herds there are gradually diminishing, and the people of Texas are turning their attention more and more from stock to agriculture. The whole number of cattle brought North in a year is about 100,000 head. Of these perhaps 20,000 go to Montana, 8000 to Utah, 8000 to Nevada, 9000 to Wyoming, 10,000 to California, 11,000 to Idaho, and 30,000 to Kansas and Colorado. The amount of capital required to transfer this number of cattle is about $1,500,000.

At Abilene, Kansas, a few years ago, 200,000 head of cattle were handled in a single season. In one month—September—60,000 head were transferred, and in another month—October—75,000 head were shipped. The cattle-trade required 100 cars per day, and a single bank in Kansas City handled during the season $3,000,000 of cattle-money. Both the Abilene, Kansas, and Schuyler, Nebraska, cattle-trade has greatly fallen off, as Chicago and St. Louis buyers now go direct to the herds and purchase, instead of as formerly sending agents to the cattle-centres. A few years ago

27,000 head changed hands in one season at Schuyler, and a bank in Omaha handled in three months $500,-000 cattle-money. General R. A. Cameron, who operates in Colorado, says: A herd of 5000 cattle will require about eight herders, at an expense of $900 per annum for two, and $600 each per annum for six, including their food; total, $5400. Allowing $2100 for incidental expenses, including teams, horses, saddles, and shanties for the men, the grand total expense would be $7500, or $1.50 per head. Again, allowing one year for breeding, and four years for the growth of the calf, a full-grown four-year-old steer, worth $20 to $30, would cost the breeder $7.50. A Texas yearling can be bought for from $7 to $10; a two-year-old for from $12 to $15, and a cow for from $15 to $25. The difference is partly in quality, but more in the time and place of purchase. New stock, just driven in, is always the lowest priced. A two-year-old heifer brought from Iowa or Missouri will bring $35, and the same grade of cows from $45 to $55. Excellent milkers will bring even more; a two-year-old Durham bull, three-fourths thoroughbred, ranges from $60 to $75, and a full-grown thoroughbred will bring from $200 to $500. In cattle-raising in Colorado, General Cameron puts the profits at 50 to 55 per cent. per annum on the capital invested, over and above all expenses and losses of every kind. Mr. J. L. Brush, a reliable gentleman of Weld County, Colorado, says: " I commenced eight years ago with a capital of $400, and I now own, as the result of the increase and my own labor, 900 head of fine cattle, besides having made considerable investments in lands from money taken from the herd. I think the average profit on capital invested in cattle will not fall short of 40 per cent. per annum over and above all expenses." Mr. R. Stolls, who lives ten miles east of Colorado Springs, says : " I began with cattle in 1861, and have owned them ever since. They do well in summer and winter in Colorado without feeding. I have just sold cattle to the amount of nearly $6000." The purchase of this herd cost $1100 three years since, and $500 two years since.

CHAPTER IV.

THE MONEY TO BE MADE.

An Investment of $25,000 for Six Years and the Probable Profits
—The Same for Five Years—The Cattle-Supply.

I HAVE often been asked what a given sum of money invested in cattle would produce to the owner in a term of say six years. Of course we might answer, that would depend very much upon the skill of the manager, and so it would; but taking it for granted that good business management was displayed, then a herd ought to yield an annual increase of at least 25 per cent. per annum.

It is a remarkable fact that a large portion of the money invested in cattle is borrowed capital, and upon this a high rate of interest is paid. A gentleman who understands the cattle business two years ago made the following proposition to the writer, with a view of buying a herd on joint account:

We start with a capital of $25,000 cash, and assume that of all three-year-olds, one-half by the next spring are cows, and the balance four-year-old steers or "beeves," also that 80 per cent. of the cows have calves that mature. We buy high-grade Durham bulls, and put them with Texas cattle that have been wintered on the Arkansas River (driven from Texas the year before) and delivered on our range in July.

ESTIMATE OF PROFITS ON AN INVESTMENT OF $25,000 IN
CATTLE.

In July, 1879.

100 yearlings @ $7	$700
200 two-year-olds @ $11.	2,200
600 cows @ $16	9,600
500 three-year-olds @ $16	8,000
100 four-year-olds @ $23	2,300
250 calves (thrown in)	
———	———
1750	$22,800

The above is about the grade an average herd would
tally out, and it is cheaper to buy out a herd than to
pick. The calves are thrown in, and those born on the
drive up are usually killed, thus reducing the number
below the ordinary 80 per cent. of increase.

Expenses.

Two herders @ $35 per month and board, say $20 per	
month, $660	$1320.00
One foreman @ $50 and board, $20	840.00
Nine horses @ $75	675.00
Grain for horses at 8 lbs. per day @ 1¼ cts. for the year	328.50
One wagon, $125; two mules and harness, $400 . .	525.00
Ranch	200.00
Mower, horse-rake, and plough	200 00
Incidental expenses	1000.00
	———
	$5088.00

We sell in November and December:

100 beeves, average 1100 lbs., @ 3 cts. per lb. . .	$3300
100 cows (old), average 900 lbs., @ 3 cts. per lb. . .	2700
Add surplus of capital	2200
	———
	$8200

This leaves us $3111.50 new capital reinvestment, and we buy 200 two-year-olds @ $15 per head,—$3000, —which leaves $111.50 for "odds and ends," or incidental expenses. The purchase of two-year-olds cost more on account of "picking them."

Second Year, 1880.

We have on hand:

Yearlings (last year's calves)	250
Two-year-olds (last year's yearlings)	100
Three-year-olds (last year's two-year-olds) . . .	400
Cows (half last year's three-year-olds)	750
Beeves (half last year's three-year-olds)	250
Calves (half-breeds), 80 per cent. increase . . .	600
	2350

Expenses.

Same as first year (two herders)	$1320.00
One extra man	660.00
Same foreman	840.00
Grain	328.50
Incidental expenses	2000.00
	$5148.50

We sell in fall:

250 beeves, average 1100 lbs., @ 3 cts. per lb. . .	$8250
50 cows, average 900 lbs., @ 3 cts. per lb. . . .	1350
	$9600

Leaving $4451.50 new capital for reinvestment, and we buy 250 three-year-olds @ $18 per head,—$4500, —and reduce our "odds and ends" fund $49.50 and will drop it. It would be a better investment to buy yearlings or two-year-olds, but the herd would wander too much with so many young cattle.

Third Year, 1881.

We have on hand:

Yearlings (last year's calves)	600
Two-year-olds (last year's yearlings)	250
Three-year-olds (last year's two-year-olds) . . .	100
Cows	900
Beeves (last year's purchase three-year-olds) . . .	154
Calves (80 per cent. of increase)	720
	*2724

The calves are all one-half to three-fourths American, and we have assumed that of the last year's purchase of 250 three-year-olds 100 are steers and 150 heifers. The 600 yearlings are "half-breeds."

Expenses.

Same as second year, say		$5000
We sell 150 beeves @ $33 per head . . .	$4950	
100 cows @ $27 per head	2700	
		$7650
Balance		$2650

Leaving us $2650 new capital for reinvestment.

We buy 140 three-year-olds @ $18	$2520
Odds and ends account	130

Fourth Year, 1882.

We have on hand:

---

* Underestimate, viz.: cattle on hand July, 1881, 2350 head; sold 300; balance on hand, 2050 head; bought 250; increase, 720 = 970 × 2050 = 3020 head, instead of 2724.

Yearlings (half-breeds) 720
Two-year-olds (half-breeds) 600
Three-year-olds (half-breeds) 250
Cows (900 = 100 × 70 × 50) 920
Beeves 120
Calves (80 per cent. increase) 736
_____
3346

Expenses.

Same as third year $5000
We sell 120 beeves, average 1100 lbs., @ 3 cts.
    per lb. $3960
100 cows, average 900 lbs., @ 3 cts. per lb.. . 2760
_____
$6720

Leaving us $1660 new capital for reinvestment. We buy 80 cows @ $20 per head,—$1600,—adding $60 to odds and ends fund. (There should be one bull to every thirty cows.)

Fifth Year, 1883.

Yearlings 736
Two-year-olds 720
Three-year-olds 600
Cows (920 × 100 × 80) 880
Beeves 250
Calves (80 per cent. increase) 704
_____
*3890

Expenses.

Same as fourth year $5000
One extra man 660
Extra incidental expenses 340
_____
$6,000

* Underestimate again, viz.: cattle on hand July, 1883, 3346 head; sold 220; leaves 3126; bought 80 cows; increase, 80 per cent., = 784 × 3126 = 3910, instead of 3890.—AUTHOR.

We sell 250 beeves, average 1100 lbs., @ 3 cts.
    per lb. $8250
150 cows, average 900 lbs., @ 3 cts. per lb. . 4050
                     —— $12,300

Balance $6,300

Leaving us $6200 new capital for reinvestment.

We buy 200 three-year-old heifers @ $18 per head . . $3600
150 three-year-old steers @ $18 per head 2700
                     ——
                     $6300

Sixth Year, 1884.

We have on hand:

Yearlings 704
Two-year-olds 736
Three-year-olds 720
Cows (880 = 150 × 200 × 300) 1230
Beeves 450
Calves (80 per cent. increase) 1084
                     ——
                     4924

Assume now that a settlement is desired and the account closed, an inventory taken, and a closing-out sale effected. The yearlings are five-eighths American, the calves are seven-eighths American, and the two-year-olds are one-half American. We have but 100 of the original cows on hand, and they are the best in the lot, as the cows that have been sold each year were the old ones or poorest to breed from. The beeves are mostly one-half breeds, will weigh more and bring better prices than common Texan cattle.

Expenses.

Same as fifth year $6000

Our inventory for closing-out sale would be as follows:

Nine horses @ $50	$450
Wagons, mules, harness, etc.	375
Ranch and good-will of range	1,000
704 yearlings @ $10	7,040
736 two-year-olds @ $16	11,776
720 three-year-olds @ $24	17,280
1230 cows @ $26	31,980
450 beeves @ $33	14,858
1084 calves @ $7	7,588
	$92,237
Original capital	$25,000
Five years' compound interest @ 7 per cent.	10,061
	$35,061
Balance	$57,278
Deduct six years' expenses	6,000
Balance*	$51,278

The interest on original capital is compounded each year and reckoned at 7 per cent. The average annual loss by death or straying, etc., is less than 3 per cent. The per cent. of cows that bear calves that mature is 84 per cent. Grain has been estimated for saddle-horses for entire year, while they will not require it over one-fourth of the time. All estimates of amounts paid out are liberal and greater than they would actually be. The cost of bulls is omitted in the estimate, as the grade

---

* Though not altered by me, it will be seen my friend was wrong in his calculations in cows and beeves, and also in his general result of net profits.

(Durham) would not cost over $50 each, and they could be had for that price any time. They are generally purchased in carload lots from farmers in Illinois or Iowa, and shipped West when yearlings. We have taken great pains to show the above estimate to cattle-breeders, and several of them said it was rather under than over what they would expect to realize from a like investment. It should be observed that in the fore-going estimate the increase is just beginning to show, and in ten years the profits would be much larger, and each year exceed the original capital. It should also be remembered the larger the original investment or original capital put into the business the greater ratio of net profits would be. (If $100,000 were invested in cattle placed on suitable ranges it would easily double itself in five years, besides paying an annual dividend of 10 per cent. Again, if $200,000 were invested in Texas cattle it would double itself in four years, and pay a semi-annual dividend of 8 per cent.) I disagreed with my friend both in his calculations and method of handling cattle, and in reply to his proposition for an investment of $25,000 on our joint account, sent him the following :

ESTIMATE OF PROFITS OF A CASH CAPITAL OF $25,000 INVESTED IN CATTLE FOR FIVE YEARS.

August, 1879, First Year.

Buy 500 yearling steers, @ $7	$3,500
500 two-year-olds, @ 12	6,000
500 three-year-olds,@ 20	10,000
Expenses: horses, camp outfit, ranch, and incidentals .	5,500
	$25,000

August, 1880, Second Year.

On hand, two-year-olds	500
three-year-olds	500
beeves	500
	1500

Sell 500 beeves, average 1000 lbs., @ 3 cts. per pound .		$15,000
Expenses	$2500	
10 per cent. interest on capital . . .	2500	
		5,000
		$10,000
Buy 1000 yearlings, @ $7		7,000
$3000 surplus capital funds		$3,000

August, 1881, Third Year.

On hand, two-year-olds	1000
three-year-olds	500
beeves	500
	2000

Sell 500 beeves, @ $30		$15,000
Expenses	$2500	
Interest	2500	
		5,000
		$10,000
Buy 800 two-year-olds, @ $12		9,600
$400 to surplus capital fund		$400

August, 1882, Fourth Year.

On hand, three-year-olds	1800
beeves	500
	2300

$60,000

50,000

$60,000

14,000

$52,000

d year, first,

and, 10 per

third, $52,000

the capital in

interest, all

be a difficult

, Nebraska,

5000 head

taken up or

bes of large

and ranges,

Sell 500 beeves, @ $30 per head	$15,000
Expenses and interest	5,000
	$10,000
Buy 500 three-year-olds, @ $20	10,000

August, 1883, *Fifth Year.*

On hand, beeves		2300
Sell 2300 beeves, @ $30		$69,000
Expenses	$5000	
Interest	2500	
		7,500
		$61,500
Deduct original capital		25,000
Net profit in five years		$36,500

This would leave a capital to begin new with greater than the original, besides the ranch, horses, etc., still on hand; the $3000 surplus capital fund could have been invested in cows to hold the range. The above estimate is based upon the supposition that $25,000 capital had been borrowed for four years at 10 per cent. interest.

Buying yearling steers and selling beeves keeps the capital more in hand, and a class of cattle that can be forced on the market with better results to the seller; and if yearlings or two-year-olds can be bought in lots to suit the purchaser, this kind of trade will show enormous profits. A herd of

2000 yearlings, @	$7.50
2000 two-year-olds, @	12.00
2000 three-year-olds, @	18.00
6000 will cost, say	$75,000
Expense of herding	6,000
Interest, at 10 per cent.	7,500
End of first year	$13,500

Sell 2000 beeves, @ $30	$60,000
Deduct interest and herding	13,500
Balance	$46,500
Buy 2000 yearlings, @ $7	14,000
	$32,500

This gives at the beginning of the second year, first, the same number and grade of cattle; second, 10 per cent. interest on original capital; and third, $32,500 net profits. This will more than double the capital in three years, besides paying 10 per cent. interest, all losses, and expenses. In a few years it will be a difficult matter to find a vacant range in Wyoming, Nebraska, or Montana suitable or capable of sustaining 5000 head of cattle. The water-courses are fast being taken up or squatted upon by small herders or branches of large herds.

If $250,000 were invested in ten ranches and ranges, placing 2000 head on each range, by selling the beeves as fast as they mature, and all the cows as soon as they were too old to breed well, and investing the receipts in young cattle, at the end of five years there would be at least 45,000 head on the ten ranges, worth at least $18 per head, or $810,000. Assuming the capital was borrowed at 10 per cent. interest, in five years the interest would amount to $125,000, which must be deducted; $250,000 principal, and interest for five years, compounded at 25 per cent. per annum, would only be $762,938, or less than the value of the cattle, exclusive of the ranches and fixtures. I have often thought if some enterprising persons would form a joint-stock company for the purpose of breeding, buying, and selling horses, cattle, and sheep it would prove enormously profitable. I have no doubt but a company properly managed would declare an annual dividend of ·at least 25 per cent. Such a company organized, with a president, secretary, treasurer, and board of directors, and conducted on strictly business principles, would realize a far larger profit on the money invested than if put into mining, lumber, iron, manufacturing, or land companies. Nothing, I believe, would beat associated capital in the cattle trade, unless it would be banking, and stock-raising would probably fully compete with even banking as a means of profit on capital invested in large sums.

Such a company should buy Texas cattle, locate them on ranges, placing 5000 head on each ranch, then breed them up for the market, increasing quantity and quality as fast as possible, selling all beeves whenever mature, and cows as fast as they become too old to breed from or were not suitable for breeding purposes. As fast as beeves and cows were sold the first three years the money realized should be used, or at least a good part of it, to fill up the herds with good young stock.

The ranches and ranges should be located with a view of ultimately buying the land or securing control of it for a long term of years. The company should operate and secure, to as great an extent as possible, the monopoly of government contracts and furnishing the Eastern markets with beef. It should aim to grow to be a controlling power in all that affected beef, and eventually, not only packed beef and pork, but tan hides and manufacture wool into cloth. It is not generally known that one-third of all the woollens used in the United States is sold west of the Mississippi River; but such is the fact, and the principal cause of this great consumption is because the climate of Colorado, Wyoming, Nebraska, Montana, and indeed all the Plains and Rocky Mountain country is so cool woollens are worn nearly the year round. The climate is admirably adapted for it, and there is no reason in the world why the largest pork and beef packeries, as well as tanneries, should not be established in the West. The beef business cannot be overdone. The census of the United States will probably show a population in 1880 of not less than 47,000,000 of people, and the cattle-raising does not keep pace with the rapid increase of population. In the Eastern and Middle States for the last ten years there has been a rapid decrease of cattle, and in a few years the West will be called on to supply almost the whole Eastern demand. Land worth over $10 per acre is too valuable to be devoted to stock-raising, and farmers can do better in cereals. It is for this reason our Eastern farmers are giving up the cattle-breeding and devoting their lands to raising corn, wheat, rye, oats, and vegetables. They cannot compete with Plains beef, for while their grazing-lands cost them $50, $75, and $100 per acre, and hay has to be cut for winter feeding, the grazing-lands in the West have no market value, and the cattle run at large all winter, the natural grasses curing on the ground and keeping the stock fat even in January, February, and March. Much of Montana, Dakota, Nebraska, Colorado, and

nearly all of Wyoming can never become an agricultural country, and the government will soon be called
upon to put the grazing-lands into market, so that our
stock-raisers may establish permanent ranches and buy
their cattle-ranges.   It will very soon be cheaper to
fence than to herd stock.   The time, I believe, is not
far distant when the West will supply the people of the
East with beef for their tables, wool for their clothing,
horses for their carriages, 'busses, and street-railways,
and gold and silver for their purses.   Horse-raising and
sheep-growing have proved to be successful enterprises
in Wyoming and Montana, and the profits are enormous.   Oregon mares can be bought at $30 per head,
blooded stallions at $500, and these bred to Oregon
mares yield a profit of 25 per cent. on the capital invested.   Sheep-farming is still more profitable, and an
investment of $5000 can be made to pay 35 per cent.
the first year, 47 per cent. the second year, and 60 per
cent. the third year.   Of these two interests I shall
speak in detail further on.

CHAPTER V.

MILLIONS IN BEEF.

An Interesting Letter from One Who Knows—A Generous Offer
of a Fortune—Just what can be done with Money and Brains
—Figures that Tell.

CONTINUING the subject of what can be made out
of a given sum of money invested in cattle-growing
out West, we cannot better estimate the increase of a
herd than by submitting a letter written by a gentleman of means to his brother in the East, whom he
wished to put into the cattle business on their joint account. The letter, which I am permitted to copy, reads
as follows:

DEAR BROTHER,—I have bought a cattle-ranch,
and as you have long wished to engage in business out
West, I do not know of a better thing you can do than
raise cattle. As you have no knowledge or experience
in breeding, I will tell you what I think, with proper
care, we can make out of it. The ranch is twenty-two
miles from a railroad, and contains 720 acres of land,
600 acres of which is hay or grass land, and 120 acres
good timber. The meadow will cut annually 2½ tons
of hay to the acre, and there is a living stream on the
land. The timber is heavy, and will furnish logs for

stables, corrals, and fuel for many years to come.
The hills in the vicinity afford the best grazing, and
we can have a range ten miles in extent. There is a
little town nine miles off, and a school-house four miles
distant. The valley in which the ranch is located is
well settled, and there is no danger from Indians.
The cattle would be grazed in the hills, and driven to
and from the ranch every day. The three great requi-
sites for a good ranch are wood, water, and grass, and
these we have in abundance. If you can sell out where
you are and bring $5000 West with you, I am sure you
will never have a better opportunity to engage in a
lucrative business. I will make you a proposition, as
follows: you can put in $2500, and I will duplicate it
and add $1000 for bulls. For $5000 we can get 400
head of Texas cows to start with, and I will add a sufficient number of Durham bulls to breed them. I will
erect all the necessary buildings, purchase machinery,
wagons, horses, etc. I will own the ranch and fixtures,
and you be at the expense of taking care of the herd
and give me half the increase. With your two boys
to help as herders, it would only be necessary at the
beginning to hire one man. The hay you could get
put up at a cost of $1 per ton, or by hiring an extra
man in haying time it would cost you 50 cents per ton.
I would put in say 200 head of Texas cows, and you
200 head. I might add, on my own account, 100 or
200 head, but if I did it would be at no expense to
you, and make no difference in the division of profits,
you having half the increase and gain of everything.
It is likely if we started with 400 head in 1877, I would

"ROUNDING OUT" THE CALVES.

in the spring of 1878 add 100 Texas two-year-old steers, and in the following spring 100 Iowa milch cows. I know what a good, thrifty, industrious soul your wife is, and you may tell her for me if she comes West I will buy her 100 fine cows for a dairy, and she can market all her butter and milk at the railroad, twenty-two miles distant, and get rich on her own account. It is the custom in the West not to put up hay or build shelter for stock in winter, but I do not believe in this. Cattle can generally be grazed out all winter, but there are some winters very severe, and not unfrequently dreadful storms, during which cattle die. Herds slip through two or three years all right, but in the end lose heavily. The loss from one storm would be more than it would cost to cut hay for ten years. Besides, my idea of a ranch is "home for man and beast," and I would rather be at some extra expense than to have the cattle suffer. The heavy timbered bottom will give all the shelter necessary, and the meadows will yield 1500 tons of hay per year, which will be all that we need to insure us against storms and hard winters. Now let us see what we can do with a herd of 400 Texas cows, worth $5000, to begin with. At the end of one year the cows would have 400 calves, each worth $7. I count full yield, for in cross-breeding there is not one cow in a hundred barren, neither is the loss over one per cent. of calves dropped where hay and shelter is provided, and proper care taken. Our first year's profit is 400 calves, $7 each, $2800, divided, $1400 each.

6

Second Year.

400 calves (old cows) @ $7	$2800
Increase value on last year's calves, they being half Durham, @ $5 each	2000
	$4800

Divided, we each have $2400.

Third Year.

400 calves (old cows) @ $7 each	$2800
Increase value on first year's calves @ $5 each . .	2000
" " second year's calves @ $5 each . .	2000
	$6800

Divided by two gives us $3400 each.

Fourth Year.

400 calves (old cows) @ $7 each	$2,800
Increase value on first year's calves @ $5 each . .	2,000
" " second year's calves @ $5 each .	2,000
" " third year's calves @ $5 each . .	2,000
First year's calves, half of which are heifers,* now come in with calves, and add 200 to the herd, worth .	1,400
	$10,200

Divided by two gives us each $5100.

Fifth Year.

400 calves (old cows) @ $7 each	$2,800
First year's heifer calves 200 @ $7	1,400
Second year's heifer calves 200 @ $7	1,400
Increase on first year's calves @ $5 each . . .	2,000
" second year's calves @ $5 each . . .	2,000
" third year's calves @ $5 each . . .	2,000
" fourth year's calves @ $5 each . . .	2,000
" last year's heifer calves 200 @ $5 each .	1,000
	$14,600

---

* The heifer would probably breed the third year, but it should be prevented as far as possible.

This year we also make our first sale, and have 200 steers
to sell, worth $30 each   6,000

Increase and cash, grand total $20,600
Divided by two, cash each $3000; in stock, $7300,
making   10,300

We now have on our ranch the following stock:

First year's cows   400
    "   calves   400
                                                 800

Second Year.

Old cows   400
First year's calves   400
Second   "   400
                                          1200

Third Year.

Old cows   400
First year's calves   400
Second   "   400
Third   "   400
                                          1600

Fourth Year.

Old cows   400
First year's calves   400
Second   "   400
Third   "   400
Fourth   "   400
Heifer calves   200
                                          2200

Fifth Year.

Old cows   400
First year's calves   400
Second   "   400
Third   "   400
Fourth   "   400
Fifth   "   400

First year's heifer calves (yearlings) 200
" " just dropped 200
Second " " " 200

——

3000

Less 200 steers sold, leaves 2800 to winter. If we sex the cattle, which is the only way to get at their value, we shall have:

First Year.

400 cows, 200 heifer calves. Total females . . . 600
Bull calves 200

——

800

Second Year.

400 cows, 200 yearling heifers, 200 heifer calves. Making
a total of females 800
200 bull yearlings, 200 bull calves 400

——

1200

Third Year.

400 cows, 200 two-year-old heifers, 200 yearling heifers,
200 heifer calves. Total females 1000
200 two-year-old steers, 200 yearlings, 200 bull calves.
Total males 600

——

1600

Fourth Year.

400 cows, 200 three-year-old heifers, 200 two-year-olds,
200 yearlings, 200 young calves, half of heifer
calves, 100. Total females 1300
200 three-year-old steers, 200 two-year-olds, 200 yearlings,
200 bull calves, half heifer calves, 100. Total males 900

——

2200

Fifth Year.

400 cows, 200 four-year-olds, 200 three-year-old heifers,
200 two-year-old heifers, 200 yearling heifers, 200
calves; also, 100 heifer calves (yearlings) from four-

year-olds, 100 from three-year-olds, and 100 from four-year-olds just come in for the second time. Total females 1700

200 four-year-old steers, 200 three-year-olds, 200 two-year-olds, 200 yearlings, 200 bull calves; alsó, from four-year-old heifers, 100 bull yearlings and 100 bull calves; also, from three-year-old heifers just come in with their calves, 100 males. Total males. . 1300

_____

3000

Deduct 200 steers sold, leaves 2800 head to be kept on hand. It will be observed that our business is just established and beginning to pay. It takes five or six years to establish any good business on a firm basis, and our ranch is now thoroughly "set up," as frontiersmen would say. After the fifth year the profits will be enormous. Let us run it the sixth year, and the account would stand something like this:

Sixth Year.

400 old cows, 400 old cows' calves,—this being their sixth dropping, and the last; 200 five-year-old cows, 200 four-year-old cows, 200 calves from five-year-old cows, 200 calves from four-year-old cows, 200 calves from three-year-old cows. We would brand 1000 calves the sixth year worth $7 each, or $7000. The increase in value on our stock would stand as follows:

The sixth year, 400 old cows' calves, worth . . . $2,800
600 five-year-old, four-year-old, and three-year-old cows' calves, worth 4,200
Increase in value on 200 four-year-old cows . . . 1,000
"   "   "   three-year-old cows   . . 1,000
"   "   "   four-year-old steers   . . 1,000
"   "   three-year-old steers   . . 1,000

6*

Increase in value on 600 two-year-olds	3,000
" " 800 yearlings	4,000
	$19,000
Sell 200 beeves, @ $30 each . . . . . .·	6,000
	$25,000
Add 200 calves, @ $7 each	1,400

Divided by two gives us each $3000 in cash and $12,500 in stock.

As our herd would now be getting too large for our ranch we would have to cut it down, and for that purpose we would sell:

400 Texas cows, full blood, @ $15 per head . . .	$6,000
200 half-blood Durhams, five-year-olds (cows), @ $22 per head	4,400
200 half-blood Durhams, four-year-olds (cows), @ $15 per head	3,000
200 half-blood Durhams, steers, @ $25 per head . .	5,000
	$18,400

Divided by two gives us $9200 each more in cash, to which we must add cash realized from sale of four-year-old steers, $6000 = $24,400 or $12,200 each in cash the sixth year. These figures may astonish you, but I assure you they are rather under than over the usual estimate, and many herders on the Plains have done better. Of course, to show the real profits, it will be necessary to make up the expense list. It will stand something like the following:

Ranch	$5,000
2 yoke cattle, $75 per yoke	150
Studebaker wagon	100
Mowing-machine	125
	$5,375

Add cost my share cattle the first year 2,500

Expenses : $7,875

Your share of cattle first year $2,500
4 herd-horses, $125 each 500
2 dogs, $30 each 60

$3,060
Add my expenses 7,875

First year, grand total $10,935
First year, increase of cattle $2800
My share 1400
Deduct 10 per cent. for loss of cattle . . $140
Wear and tear of machinery, etc. . . . 200
340

My actual profit first year $1100
Your share 1400
Deduct 10 per cent. for loss of cattle . . $140
Hire of Indian herder, $10 per month . . . 120
To putting up 800 tons of hay . . . 400
660

Your actual profits first year $740

Second Year.

Your account—Increase of herd $2400
Expense of herder $120
1000 tons of hay 500
Loss of cattle, 10 per cent. . . . 240
860

Your actual profits $1540

My account—Increase of cattle $2400
Expense, wear of machinery, etc. . . . $200
Loss of cattle, 10 per cent. 240
440

My actual profits $1960

Third Year.

Your account—Increase of cattle		$3400
Expense, 2 herders	$240	
Loss of cattle, 10 per cent.	340	
1500 tons of hay	750	
		1330
Your actual profits		$2070
My account—Increase of cattle		$3400
Wear of machinery, etc.	$200	
Loss of cattle, 10 per cent.	340	
		540
My actual profits		$2860

Fourth Year.

Your account—Increase of cattle		$5100
Expenses, 3 herders	$360	
2000 tons of hay	1000	
Loss on cattle, 10 per cent. . . .	510	
		1870
Your actual profits		$3230
My account—Increase of cattle		$5100
Expenses, wear of machinery, etc. . .	$200	
Loss on cattle, 10 per cent. . . .	510	
		710
My actual profits		$4390

Fifth Year.

Your account—Increase of cattle . . .	$7300	
Sales of beef	3000	
		$10,300
Expenses, 4 herders	$480	
3000 tons of hay	1500	
Loss on cattle, 10 per cent. . . .	1030	
		3,010
Your actual profits		$7,290

My account—Increase of cattle . . .	$7300		
Sales of beef	3000		
	——	$10,300	
Expenses, wear of machinery . . .	$200		
Loss on cattle, 10 per cent.	1030		
	——	1,230	
My actual profit		$9,070	

As I originally put in $7875, in five years my annual income is greater than my original investment; but you have done still better, for having originally invested only $3060 your income from it annually is $7290, or more than double your investment. If we undertake to keep down the herd and not let it increase, the profits will double again. What business on earth is there that can equal this? In my estimate I have said nothing about taxes, but as they are trifling, and I would pay them, they need not enter into our account. At the end of six years, if all went well in our business, I would propose a change. We could safely count on realizing from sales $10,000 a year, and certainly $8000. The first year after the sixth we would erect better buildings, and the second year (eighth after beginning) we would buy land and add to our ranch. The third year (ninth) we would buy blooded-stock cows, and the fourth (tenth) blooded horses and mares. The fifth year we would close out all our common stock, and keep nothing but blooded animals. This year, also, I would sell out to you the ranch, stock, fixtures, and everything, you to pay me $10,000 a year until all was paid up. You have often said you wished me to put you into a good business and show you how to make some money, and now, sir, I think I have pointed you out the way to a fortune, and the good wife too. In eleven years you can, by care, be at the head of a blooded-stock farm worth $100,000, and very soon afterwards its sole owner.

The above letter is remarkable, inasmuch as it is written by a gentleman to his brother, who is already in business, and advises him to come West and engage in cattle-growing. The writer of the letter has made a great deal of money, and takes this method of helping his brother to a fortune. It is likely the business-man gave the whole cattle-trade a careful investigation before advising a brother with a family to leave his comfortable farm in the East and engage in ranching cattle out West. There are some singular features about the letter, and I asked the author after reading it how he could possibly expect to get more for old Texas cows than he originally paid for them. His reply was, "I would buy young cows, say two-year-olds, and they would grow. I would fatten them and sell them for beef. I am doing it every year." I asked him, "Why would you not allow the first lot of female calves to breed at three years old?" He replied, "I think the stock would be better if the heifers were not let get with calf until after they were three years old; at all events, I wished my brother to try it and see." "How would you prevent them from breeding?" "Bulls should always be kept in a separate pasture, and not allowed to run with the herd. The cows should be put in to them at night. A good bull will serve five or six cows in a single night. The Durham bull puts a strong impress on his calves, and the first cross with a Texas

cow will produce a calf nearly two-thirds Durham."
" In the commencement of your letter you say you
would in 1879 add 100 two-year-old Texas steers to the
herd. Why do you do that?" " So as to realize sooner
from the ranch. In two years they would be full-
grown beeves, and sell, at $30 each, for $6000. If I
could put in 200 three-year-olds it would be still better,
for then we could realize on them the very next year.
On my brother's account, he being poor, I wish the
ranch to begin paying as soon as possible." " Why,
then, do you make him buy herd-horses at $125 each,
when ponies can be had at $40 per head?" " Because
he should use mares and raise colts. I would give him
a stallion, and with five good Kentucky mares, which
he could bring out with him, he could soon have a fine
lot of colts. On a stock ranch everything should be
made to increase and multiply. Why, even the two
dogs, one should be a bitch and raise shepherd pups,
and those raised on the ranch would be far more valuable for herding than imported dogs." " You say you
would buy 100 Iowa cows and have the women start a
dairy?" " Yes. The way to get rich is for every one to
work. My ranch is twenty-two miles from the Union
Pacific Railroad, over which every year butter is shipped
to the Pacific coast. Why, do you know, as many as
five car-loads of butter were shipped from Omaha to
California in one day. This butter comes from Iowa,
and I don't see why the people living west of Iowa
should not supply the California market. But there is
a better thing to do with butter than to send it to the
Pacific coast. There is Fort Hartsuff, Fort Russell,

Bridger, Laramie, Fetterman, and Sidney Barracks, and the soldiers want good butter. The officers and commissaries send all the way East to Ohio, Pennsylvania, and New York, in order to get the best butter. Now, the lady I propose to give the Iowa cows to is a buttermaker, one of the best, indeed, in the country, and I shall advise her to pack and ship to the forts, where she will always find a ready market for all she can make." " I notice you propose to use Indians as herders ; are they good for that purpose ?" " The best in the world. The Pawnee Indian is a natural Lerder, and if I had a million head of cattle I would place them all under Pawnee herders; half-breeds if I could get them." "In your sixth year's estimate you speak of adding 200 calves. Where do you get them from ?" " You forget that we have been in business six years, and our second generation, or three-year-olds, are coming in with calves,—that is to say, a cow that has a female calf. Now, in three years the calf will have a calf. In cattle-raising the herd doubles up and dovetails so fast it is with difficulty we can compute increase, but I guess you will find my figures about correct." This gentleman was so very clear and intelligent in all his answers, he satisfied me entirely that he knew what he was about, and not only understood the cattle business, but mining, sheep-farming, horse-growing, and many other businesses common to the West.

CHAPTER VI.

GREAT LANDS IN THE SOUTHWEST.

Texas Cattle-Kings—Who They Are and What They Own—
Mammoth Ranches—Letters from Cattle-Owners on the
Plains—Cattle-Grasses.

I HAVE often been asked to write something about
the great cattle-herds of Texas. As yet we have but
few herds in the West, the business being too new.
An owner with 10,000 or 12,000 head in Wyoming or
Montana would be considered a large grower, but such
a person in New Mexico or Texas a few years ago,
when I was there, would have been called but a small
herder. I do not think the herds South are as large
or numerous now as they were five years since, and the
business is gradually drawing off North to the Plains,
which are the natural homes of the future cattle-kings
of America. Texas, in 1867, had 2,000,000 of oxen
and other cattle, exclusive of cows. In 1870 it was
estimated the number had increased to 3,000,000, exclusive of cows, and of these there were 80,000 in the
State returned by the county assessors. The enormous total of 3,800,000 cattle in one State may well
excite our astonishment. Of these, one-fourth were
beeves, one-fourth cows, and the other two-fourths
yearlings and two-year-olds. The increase each year
was 750,000 calves, and of the older cattle there was

on hand at one time 1,900,000 young cattle, 950,000 cows, and 950,000 beeves. These cattle were scattered along the Nucces, Guadalupe, San Antonio, Colorado, Leon, Brazos, Trinity, Sabine, and Red Rivers. Colonel Richard King, on the Santa Catrutos River, was one of the largest owners. His ranch, known as the Santa Catrutos ranch, contained nineteen Spanish leagues of land, or about 84,132 acres. The Santa Catrutos River and its tributaries water this immense ranch, and on it were grazing 65,000 head of cattle, 10,000 horses, 7000 sheep, and 8000 goats. 1000 saddle-horses and 300 Mexicans were kept constantly employed in herding, sorting, and driving the stock. The number of calves branded annually on this ranch were 12,000 head, and the number of beeves sold about 10,000. Near Golaid, on the San Antonio River, is located Mr. O'Connor's ranch. Some years ago he had 40,000 head of cattle, and branded annually 11,700 calves. The sales of beeves amounted to from $75,000 to $80,000 per year. Mr. O'Connor commenced cattle-raising with 1500 head, for which he paid $8000, in 1852. Mr. Kennedy's ranch on the Rio Grande and Nueces contained 142,840 acres. A fertile little peninsula jutted into the Gulf, and was surrounded on three sides by water. The other side was closed with plank, the whole line of fence being 30 miles long. Every three miles there was a little ranch by the fence, and a house for the Mexican herders. On the ranch there were 30,000 head of cattle, besides an immense number of other stock. There were many other large ranches on the Rio Grande, Nueces, Guadalupe, San Antonio,

Colorado, Leon, Brazos, Trinity, Sabine, and Red Rivers. Mr. John Hitson had 50,000 head of cattle on a ranch in Pinto County, on the Brazos. He drove 10,000 head North annually, and employed 300 saddle-horses and 50 herders to take care of his cattle. Twenty years ago he was working by the day on a Texas farm. John Chisholm had 30,000 head; Mr. Parks, 20,000; James Brown, 15,000; Martin Childers, 10,000; Robert Sloan, 12,000; Mr. Coleman, 12,000; Charles Rivers, 10,000; and many others from 8000 to 20,000 head. These were some of the cattle-princes of Texas. Of the 1000 men who owned 3,000,000 head of cattle, it is said not one hundred commenced with large means. Texas is fast becoming an agricultural State, and in a few years more most of the great herds there will be transferred to the Plains of the West, the natural grazing-grounds of the nation.

Among the great drivers North are John Hitson, who brings up from Texas to the Plattes every year 7000 to 8000 head; John Chisholm, 6000; James Patterson, 8000; George F. Reynolds, 5000; Charles Goodnight, 5000; John Anderson, 3000; W. P. Black, 2000; C. C. Campbell, 3000; Robert White, 2000; Samuel Goldstone, 2000; Henry Martin, 2000; and many others from 1000 to 4000 head. The whole number of cattle driven North from Texas annually cannot be less than 100,000 to 150,000. The superior advantages of the Northern climate over the South for cattle has become so generally known as to need no comment. I will not, therefore, give my own opinion, but those of men more competent to judge.

Dr. Latham says: "All the country west of Omaha, on the line of the Union Pacific Railroad, as far as Fort Kearney is in the belt where twenty-five inches of rain falls yearly. West of Fort Kearney, extending to the Sierra Madre, on this railroad line, including the Black Hills and Laramie Plains, is the belt where twenty inches fall annually, with the exception of a small portion of country in Texas, called the Staked Plain. These two belts include all the trans-Missouri country west, from the Missouri and Mississippi to the snowy range. This rainfall includes the snow reduced to water measure, twelve inches of snow making one inch of water. This water falls mostly in the spring in gentle rains, during the month of May, which is the rainy season of the country. In the month of May the rain gives our grasses their growth, and by June 1st to 15th they are fully matured. Our rains then come in short showers, and the fall for the summer is small. Our grasses begin to cure, and by September 1st they have become perfectly cured uncut hay. This one fact alone is the key to the great superiority of this country for grazing. Our grasses cure instead of decomposing, as there is neither heat nor moisture, both of which are necessary for the chemical process of decomposition.

"As you leave the Missouri River you enter the belt of country where two feet of snow falls. This belt extends, like the first belt of rain, to Fort Kearney. West of that point to the mountain's foot is the belt of eighteen inches. The snowfalls at a single storm are very light, three inches being exceptionally large, and this amount being dry and light never lies on a level; in twenty-four hours from the time of fall the ground is bare."

Dr. Charles Alden, formerly post surgeon at Fort D. A. Russell, writes: "During the months of March, April, September, November, and December, 1868, the amount of snowfall was 4.37 inches, the greatest being in March, 1.6 inches. The records of the year 1869 are more complete. There fell 13.56 inches of snow during the months of January, February, March, April, October, November, and December. The greatest amount was in March, 3.97 inches; the least in December, .13 of an inch. The snow in this vicinity rapidly disappears after falling, and it is very rare that there is a sufficient quantity or that it remains long enough to give sleighing. During the winter season proper, though the thermometer sometimes sinks to ten or fifteen degrees below zero, the weather is usually clear and open and the roads good. There are not only the 'bunch' and 'gramma' grasses, but a thousand other species. Each valley has its complement of species."

Dr. Corey writes: "During the summer of 1865 I travelled northwest of Omaha, following up the Loup Fork of the Platte, leaving which we crossed Niobrara, north and south forks of the Big Cheyenne River, thence following along the base of the eastern Black Hills, thence still northwest across the Little Missouri, and then down the Powder River to the Yellowstone. Our route returning was along the base of the Big Horn Mountains and the Black Hills, and down the Platte. The grazing the whole distance of this jour-

ney, which was not less than sixteen hundred miles,
was good.   There is considerable land which does not
grow grass, such as some places in the Mauvais Terre.
Yet there is grass in all the country we passed over for
countless herds of cattle, sheep, and horses.   Buffalo,
elk, antelope, and deer, in immense numbers, graze
here both summer and winter.   Old mountaineers,
hunters, and trappers all told me that the winter
grazing was fine, and uninterrupted by snow.   I have
been familiar with the winter grazing in that country for
six winters, and I am sure that stock will winter on the
native grass without shelter as well as they do in Illinois with shelter and with hay and grain."

J. W. Iliff (deceased), the great cattle-owner of Wyoming, wrote: "I have been engaged in the stock business in Colorado and Wyoming for the past fourteen
years.   During all that time I have grazed stock in
nearly all the valleys of these Territories, both summer
and winter.   The cost of both summering and wintering is simply the cost of herding, as no feed nor shelter
is required.   I consider the summer-cured grass of
these plains and valleys as superior to any hay.   My
cattle have not only kept in good order on this grass
through all the light winters, but many of them, thin
in the fall, have become fine beef by spring.   During
this time I have owned over 20,000 head of cattle.
The percentage of loss in wintering here is much less
than in the States, where cattle are stabled and fed on
corn and hay.   The cost of raising cattle here can be
shown from the fact that I would be glad to contract
to furnish any quantity of beef, from heavy, fat cattle,

in Chicago at seven cents, net weight. My experience in sheep has not been so extensive as in cattle. I think, however, that the short, sweet grass and the dry climate here is especially adapted to raising sheep. I am confident, from my experience, that this trans-Missouri country can defy all competition in the production of wool, mutton, beef, and horses."

Alexander Major says: "I have been grazing cattle on the Plains and in the mountains for twenty years. I have during that time never had less than 500 head work-cattle, and for two winters, those of 1857 and 1858, I wintered 1500 head of heavy work-oxen on the Plains each winter. My experience extends from El Paso, on the Rio Grande, to one hundred miles north of Fort Benton, Montana. Our stock is worked hard during the summer, and comes to the winter herding-ground thin. Then it is grazed without shelter, hay and grain being unknown. By spring the cattle are all in good working order, and many of them fat enough for beef. I have often sold as high as $33\frac{1}{2}$ per cent. of a drove of work-oxen for beef that were thin the fall before, that had fattened on the winter grass. During these twenty years the firm with which I was connected wintered many cattle in Missouri and Arkansas on hay and corn, and I am sure the percentage of loss of those wintered in this country in all the valleys of the trans-Missouri country is less than it was in the States with food and shelter. From my twenty years' experience, I say without hesitation that all the country west of the Missouri River is one vast pasture, affording unequalled summer and winter pasturage, where sheep, cattle, and horses can be raised with only the cost of herding."

James A. Moore, now deceased, said: " I am familiar with grazing for eleven years. I have grazed stock each and every summer and winter during that time. I have had experience with horses, sheep, and cattle. I have found no difficulty in wintering stock without shelter other than is afforded by the bluffs and in the cañons. My loss in winter has been less than during my experience in stock-raising in Ohio. I have now 8000 sheep which have been wintered well on native grasses. Since bringing them to this cool and elevated country they have increased in the quantity as well as quality of the wool. I know of no disease which prevails among sheep in this country. Out of 8000 head I have lost only two this winter by wolves. I think this country peculiarly the home of sheep. I can raise wool here for less than one-half what it can be raised in Ohio or other Eastern States."

CHAPTER VII.

MORE ABOUT CATTLE-LANDS.

Interesting Letters—The Testimony of Generals Reynolds, Myers, and Bradley, Edward Creighton, Alexander Street, and Governors McCook and Campbell—The Future of the Plains.

THIS chapter is a continuation of the subject-matter treated in my last. I will proceed by giving an extract from General Reynolds's " Explorations of the Yellowstone," pages 74 and 75:

" Through the whole of the season's march the subsistence of our animals had been obtained by grazing after we had reached camp in the afternoon, and for an hour or two between the dawn of day and our time of starting. The consequence was that when we reached our winter quarters there were but few animals in the train that were in a condition to have continued the march without a generous diet. Poorer or more brokendown creatures it would be difficult to find. They were at once driven up the valley of Deer Creek, and herded during the day and brought to camp and kept in a corral through the night. In the spring all were in as fine condition for commencing another season's work as could be desired. A greater change in their appearance could not have been produced, even if they had

f

been grain-fed and stable-housed all winter. Only one
was lost, the furious storm of December coming on before it had gained sufficient strength to endure it. This
fact that 70 exhausted animals turned out to winter on
the Plains on the 1st of November came out in the
spring in the best condition, and with the loss of but
one of the number, is the most forcible commentary I
can make upon the quality of the grass and the character of the winter."

General William Myers, United States Army, writes:
" I have had some experience with stock on the Plains
and the mountains for the past four winters. Quarter-
masters' animals, horses, and mules have grazed more
or less at the following posts each of the winters of 1866,
1867, 1868, 1869, and since, viz.: Forts Kearney,
McPherson, and Sidney Barracks, Nebraska; Forts
Sedgwick and Morgan, Colorado; Forts Laramie, Fetterman, Reno, Phil Kearney, Saunders, D. A. Russell,
Fred Steele, and Bridger, Wyoming Territory; Camp
Douglass, in Utah; and Fort C. F. Smith, in Montana.
These forts embrace a country five hundred miles north
and south, and eight hundred miles east and west. I
am of the opinion that in consequence of the peculiar
nutritious grasses, and the lightness of the snowfalls in
all this extent of country, herds of sheep, cattle, and
horses can be grazed the year round with perfect safety
from danger in winter, and with great profit."

General L. P. Bradley, an excellent judge, writes:
" I know the country on the east slope of the moun-
tains from the Big Horn down to the Republican and
Smoky Hill, which I prospected or scouted pretty

thoroughly. From the Smoky Hill, in about latitude
39° north to latitude 44° the country is very much like
that immediately around the Union Pacific Railroad,
with which you and the travelling public are familiar.
The character of all this country is rolling prairie, very
well watered, and abounding in good grasses to such an
extent that the assertion may be safely made that the
supply of grazing is unlimited. All the streams in this
range furnish some timber, and many of the tributaries
of the Republican, Powder, Tongue, Big Horn, and
other rivers are covered with forests of hard- and soft-
wood. All of the bottom-lands on the streams flowing
from the mountains are what would be called in the
East good, reliable farming-lands, fit to produce any
of the regular crops, except perhaps corn. The only
danger to the corn-crop would be, I suppose, the short-
ness of the season and the frequency of frosts conse-
quent on the extreme altitude of this section. North
of latitude 44° the country changes materially for the
better. It is better watered, having an abundance of
pure, clear mountain streams. The soil is richer, and
the grasses are heavier and stronger, and the climate
very much milder than that for several degrees south.
I think the valleys of Tongue River, Little Horn, Big
Horn, and the Yellowstone will produce corn, and good
corn, too. About the other crops, barley, wheat, potatoes, etc., there is no question. This, I take it, shows
about the maximum of soil and climate, for there is no
question about the value of a country that embraces
hundreds of millions of acres that will produce good
crops of cereals and grasses."

The valley of the Big Horn, five to twenty miles in width by about one hundred miles in length, I regard as one of the choice spots of the earth. Here the climate, soil, scenery, and natural productions combine to make a country I have not seen excelled anywhere from Georgia to Montana, and equalled only by the favored countries along the Ohio, the Cumberland, or the Tennessee. The prevailing winds are westerly, bringing the mild airs of the Pacific to these inland slopes, and tempering the winters of latitude 45° and 46° to about the temperature of the mountain country of Kentucky and Tennessee. The value of this country for grazing may be estimated from the fact that good fine grasses grow evenly all over the country; that the air is so fine that the grasses cure on the ground without losing any of their nutriment, and that the climate is so mild and genial that stock can range and feed all the winter, and keep in excellent condition without artificial shelter or fodder. The fact of grasses curing on the ground is a well-known peculiarity of all the high country on the east slope of the mountains, and in this is found the great value of this immense range for grazing purposes. The difference between grasses which have to be cut and cured and those which are preserved on the ground is enough to convince the stock-raiser and herder of the value of these immense ranges known as the Plains. I believe that all the flocks and herds in the world could find ample pasturage on these unoccupied plains and the mountain slopes beyond, and the time is not far distant when the largest flocks and herds will be found right here, where the grass grows and ripens untouched from one year's end to the other. I believe there is no place in this section of the country, from latitude 47° down, where cattle and sheep will not winter safely with no feed but what they will pick up, and with only the rudest shelter. In the mountains or in the valleys of the mountain streams they would find ample shelter from storms in the frequent cañons and ravines. The mountain ranges are peculiarly adapted to sheep-raising; the range is unlimited, the grasses are fine, and the air is pure and dry,—conditions which insure healthier stock and better wool than the climate and soil of the low country. I have said that the climate about Big Horn was very mild. As an indication of this I will state that the average temperature in the valley, latitude 45° 30′, was, in December, 1867, 32° above; in January, 1868, 30° above; in February, 40° above; and in March, 55° above. In August, 1867, the mercury was as high as 107° above. Coal, iron, and fine building-stone are plentiful in the mountains of the Big Horn ranges. Fine clay and limestone are found in abundance, and the mountains furnish good pine timber in fair quantity. Nature has provided most liberally for the wants of civilization in this favored region, and when it is opened up to settlement it will attract a large population, and will prove to be a great producing country."

Edward Creighton, the great millionaire cattle-owner of Nebraska, wrote, not long before his death, as follows: "My first grazing in the country was in the winter of 1859; since then for many winters I have grazed more or less stock, including horses, sheep, and cattle, in Colorado, Wyoming, Utah, and Montana. The first seven winters I grazed work-oxen mostly. Large work-cattle winter on the grasses in the valleys and on the plains exceedingly well, and are in good condition for summer work by the first of May. The last four winters I have been raising stock, and have had large herds of cows and calves. The present winter I have wintered about 8000 head. They have done exceedingly well. We have lost very few through the whole winter, and those lost were very thin when winter commenced. We have no shelter but the bluffs and hills, no feed but the wild grasses of the country. We have had 3000 sheep the past winter, and they are in the best of order. Many are being sold daily for mutton. Like the cattle, they require no feed nor shelter. The high rolling character of the country and the dry climate, and the short, sweet grasses of the numerous hillsides, are extremely favorable to sheep-raising and wool-growing. I have been interested in stock-raising in the States for a number of years, where we had tame-grass pastures, and tame grass, hay, and fenced fields and good shelter for the stock, and good American and blooded cattle, and an experienced stock-raiser to attend to them, and after a full trial I have found out that, with the disadvantage of the vastly inferior Texas cattle, and no hay nor grain nor shelter, —nothing but the wild grass,—there is three times the profit in grazing on the Plains, and I have, as a consequence, determined to transfer my interest in stock-raising in the States to the Plains. There is no prospective limit to the pasturage west of the Missouri River. All the wool, mutton, beef, and horses that the commerce and population of our great country will require a hundred years hence, when the population is as dense as that of Europe, can be produced in this country, and at half the present prices."

Alexander Street, of Wells-Fargo Express Company, says: "From an experience of over twelve years in wintering stock on the Plains I am satisfied there is no country better adapted to the purpose than Wyoming and Colorado Territories. I have wintered herds of my own and others in Wyoming repeatedly, and the percentage of loss is less than wintering in the States on corn and hay. Here we feed nothing, but herd our stock on dry grass. During the last winter I had charge of 2000 head of cattle belonging to Wells, Fargo & Co. These cattle were worked very hard during the summer and fall in transporting government supplies to the Powder River country, and many of them were not turned out until the 1st of January, and were so poor that they could scarcely travel to the herd-ground, some forty miles. They had nothing all winter but grass, not a mouthful of hay nor grain, and yet we lost but about 30 head out of the 2000. Many of them were fat enough for beef in March and April, and by the 1st of May nearly all were in good working condition. From long experience I am fully satisfied that the gramma or bunch grass, which abounds in this country, is far superior to any of the tame grasses of the States; drying up in the fall without any rain upon it, it retains all the nutritious properties through the winter."

Speaking of the advantages of cattle- and sheep-growing in Colorado, General McCook writes : " The grasses throughout the whole Territory are so abundant and so nutritious that stock-raising is destined to be óne of the most essential elements of our permanent prosperity. The natural increase of sheep in the Territory is 100 and of cattle 80 per cent. per annum. And as there is almost no limit to the pastoral capabilities of the country, so there should be no limit to the increase of stock. The natural grasses of our hills or valleys are equal in nutritious qualities to the Hungarian or other cultivated grasses of the East, and their abundance is such that the herds of a dozen States could here find pasturage ; and the winters are so mild that shelter or hay is unnecessary."

Governor Campbell, of Wyoming, in a message to the Legislature of that Territory, said : " In the chosen home of the buffalo and the other graminivorous animals, which have for unnumbered years roamed over our Plains and subsisted upon their succulent and nutritious grasses, it would seem superfluous to say anything in relation to our advantages as a stock-growing country, or the wisdom or propriety of passing such laws as will give protection to herds and flocks, and thus encourage our people to engage in pastoral pursuits. In a climate so mild that horses, cattle, and sheep and goats can live in the open air through all the winter months, and fatten on the dry and apparently withered grasses of the soil, there would appear to be scarcely a limit to the number that could be raised. There is an old Spanish proverb that ' wherever the foot of the sheep touches the land turns into gold,' and the dry, gravelly soil of our Plains is peculiarly adapted for raising sheep, for while it produces the richest of grasses for their consumption, it is of a character that preserves their feet from the diseases most fatal to the flocks. As it is well known that the finer wools are grown at great altitudes, we should be able to supply the world with almost unlimited quantities of the best wool. While it may be justly deemed a reproach to the country at large that the United States has been for years past an importer of wool to the average amount of 50,000,000 pounds per annum, it is a source of satisfaction to us to know that there is a ready market at our doors, among our own countrymen, for so large an amount of all that we can grow. It is not sheep alone of the wool-bearing animals that can be made so profitable on our Plains. Our mountain ranges are in many respects reduplications of the country in which the most valuable and delicate varieties of the Cashmere and Angora goats are raised, and those flocks which browse on the shrubs growing at high altitudes in the rare high atmosphere of the mountains invariably produce the largest and finest fleece. The importation of these goats into our Territory should be encouraged. Unnumbered cattle must be raised and fattened on our soil, and with the cheap railroad freights which we have a right to expect, the herdsman of our Plains, while advancing his own fortune, will prove a benefactor to the laboring classes of the East, by bringing the price of the best beef within the limit of their means."

Many other letters and documents from persons

capable of judging about "Cattle-Growing out West" are before me, but these will suffice. Highly as Nebraska, Wyoming, and Colorado have been spoken of for herd-lands, still, if I was engaged in the business, I would not go to either place, for I think I know a better cattle-country. Montana has undoubtedly the best grazing-grounds in America, and parts of Dakota stand next. The Yellowstone, Big Horn, Tongue River, and Powder River regions contain the maximum of advantages to the cattle-grower. Except on the Upper Yellowstone few herds are yet located in Eastern Montana, but in the future the O'Connors, Kings, Kennedys, Hitsons, and Chisholms of the West will be found on the Yellowstone, Big Horn, and Powder River countries of Montana.

SHEEP-FARMING IN THE WEST.

SHEEP-FARMING IN THE WEST.

CHAPTER VIII.

GREAT OPPORTUNITIES.

The Raising of Sheep—Where it is Done—The Wool Crop of the World—Sheep-Walks of the Plains—A Fortune in a Clip.

SHEEP love a high and dry climate, and the higher and drier the soil the better it is for them. The countries which they mostly inhabit are Great Britain, Germany, France, Spain, Italy, Portugal, Russia, Australia, South America, South Africa, the United States, North America, Asia, and North Africa. Of these countries Great Britain has a yearly production of 260,000,000 pounds of wool; Germany, 200,000,000; France, 123,000,000; Spain, Italy, and Portugal, 119,000,000; European Russia, 125,000,000; Australia, South America, and South Africa, 250,000,000; United States, 100,000,000; North American Provinces, 10,000,000; Asia, 470,000,000; North Africa, 49,000,000.

It will be observed that the European production is 827,000,000 pounds, and the annual yield of the whole

world 1,706,000,000. The enormous value of this
wool is shown by the fact that in one year Australia
exported £30,000,000 sterling worth of wool, or about
$150,000,000 in gold, and for ten years past her trade
has been steadily increasing. Those unfamiliar with
Australia can never estimate the importance of such a
country and the effect produced upon it by an enormous
wool trade. It is the asylum for broken-down Eng-
lishmen, and in a few years they grow rich in sheep,
and generally return to the Continent to live at their
ease. Wool gives the principal prosperity to Australia,
and she now has cities larger than New Orleans with a
trade greater than Boston, Baltimore, Pittsburg, Cleve-
land, Buffalo, or Detroit. Melbourne ten or fifteen
years ago had a population of 170,000 souls, and
Sydney was as important.

In the production of the world's wool the United
States makes rather a mean figure with its 100,000,000
pounds, and it is most encouraging to wool-growers to
know we are oftentimes still heavy importers. In
1870 we imported wool and woollens to the value of
$42,229,385; and the year before, while we exported
$82,238,773 worth of breadstuffs, we sent out only
$315,881 worth of wool,—not enough to pay the duty
on our imported playing-cards. All our breadstuffs
cost three-fifths of their value to lay them down at the
sea-coast, and it may seem strange that our producers
do not raise more wool and less grain. This, however,
has its explanation in the fact that on small farms in
the East, where population is dense, farmers are compelled to raise clover for animal food, and sheep are

utterly destructive to that kind of grass. They eat the heart out of clover and the plant dies, so that the most thrifty farmers who manure their land by ploughing down clover in Ohio, Pennsylvania, and New York have almost entirely ceased to raise sheep, believing the profit to be derived from them will not pay for the injury done their lands.

The importance of wool as a source of natural wealth is shown by its effect on the increase of population and wealth where sheep are most raised. Roubaix, France, rose from a population of 5000 souls and a manufactory of 3000 pieces to 55,000 people and 400,000 pieces. Rheims began, in 1801, the manufacture of merino, and in 1863 had 55,000 workmen running 170,000 spindles and 19,000 hand-looms, annually producing 80,000,000 francs worth of cloth. Bedarieux, from a small village, has grown to be a great city, and sends out annually 250,000 pieces of cap cloth. Elbeuf, also, once a small hamlet, now has 24,000 workmen employed. Verviers, Belgium, from 5000 people has grown to 40,000 by the manufacture of cloth. In one season she sent out 70,000,000 francs worth. West Riding of Yorkshire, England, from 59,000 souls has increased to 1,375,000; Halifax, from 63,000 to 130,000; Huddersfield, from 14,000 to 38,000; Leeds, from 53,000 to 152,000; Bradford, from 14,000 to 100,000. It is in Bradford that the great English worsted-works are located.

" Not guarded Colchis gave admiring Greece
So rich a treasure in its golden fleece."

Sheep will grow almost anywhere, as is evidenced by the fact that the following countries have raised and exported wool to the United States alone: England, Scotland, Dominion of Canada, West Indies, British Africa, British East Indies, Australia, Cuba, France, Brazil, China, Argentine Republic, Dutch West Indies, Guiana, Mexico, Italy, Venezuela, Belgium, United States of Colombia, Uruguay, Russia on the Black Sea, Chili, Denmark, Danish West Indies, Austria, and Turkey. These countries embrace almost every climate on the globe, and the sheep is indeed a rare animal to adapt itself so readily to all circumstances. The finest merino wool is grown in Spain, France, Algeria, Cape Colony, on the La Plata, and in Australia.

As observed at the commencement of this chapter, the best climate for sheep is high, dry lands, where little rain falls; and generally the higher the lands the rarer the air, and the drier the climate the better will sheep thrive.

In Asia sheep are grazed 15,000 feet above the level of the sea; but, while this is true, we must not forget that they also range in Holland below the level of the sea. I am told, however, none of the diseases, such as dry-rot, balling, scab, and foot-rot, so common in low countries, prevail in the high latitudes.

The principal advantage of sheep land is in the fact it will raise sheep when it will not produce cereals or roots. The colonists in Africa, when they found they could not farm, turned their attention to wool-growing, and soon became thriving communities. The high and dry plains of South America, where little rain falls for ten months in the year, export 100,000,000 pounds of wool annually. It is there the celebrated "mestiza" is grown, from which the finest cloth is made, and so great is the demand for it that not over one-twentieth of what is needed is produced. The whole of the interior of Australia is a high table-land, where little rain falls, and from thence comes the fine fibre merino wool, from which French broadcloths and French merinos are manufactured. New Zealand, much the same as Australia, gives us the delaine wools. The lower the lands and coarser the herbage, the coarser are the wools, and the higher the soil and finer the grass, the finer are the fleeces. " The Great American Desert" is the natural home of the sheep. West of the Missouri there are 1,000,000,000 acres of land on which sheep can probably be grazed better and to more advantage than any other country in the world. Commencing at Grand Island, on the Union Pacific Railroad, one hundred and fifty miles west of Omaha, the grazing-belt, eight hundred miles wide, extends west over one thousand miles. On this enormous tract of land all the sheep in the world might be placed, and still there would be room for more. To attempt any particular description of so large a country would be impossible, and only a few of the largest ranges can be noticed. The North, South, and Middle Loup Rivers are over two hundred miles long, and flowing together, just north of Grand Island, empty a short distance below, at the city of Columbus, into the Platte River. I have been all over this region, and never saw a finer one on earth. Imagine a broad valley, green as the sea, a wide river, fringed with trees, flowing down its centre, and here and there an island covered with dense forest; little green valleys that conduct silvery streams toward their ocean home; distant hills, with bonnets blue, a glorious canopy of bright and balmy skies overspreading the whole. What scene could be more sublime? And such was the North Loup as I saw it a few years ago. At one point for fifteen miles I could look up the valley, and the prospect was unbroken, except by fields of golden grain and green waving corn. High bluffs and deep ravines filled with timber flanked the wide valley, while every two or three miles streams came leaping from the hills, meandered fantastically across the valley, and plunged into the broad river. No sweeter or more picturesque landscape ever was presented to the vision of a painter than the North Loup, the loveliest valley of the Plains. There were no cataracts, geysers, or glaciers, but thousands of patches of green earth, terraced by the hand of nature more beautiful than art could possibly have made them; quiet vales, through which rivulets flowed on forever in shade and sunlight; groves by the side of crystal pools; and hazy, golden days nine months out of every twelve in the year.

It was of this very country Bayard Taylor wrote: "I am more than ever struck with the great difference between the Great West region and the country east of the Mississippi. There is none of the wearisome monotony of the level plains, as in Illinois, or the swampy tracts, as in Indiana or Ohio. The wide, billowy green, dotted all over with golden islands of harvests;

the hollows of dark, glittering maize; the park-like clumps of timber along the course of streams,—these are the materials which make up every landscape, and of which, in their sweet, harmonious, pastoral beauty, the eye never grows weary."

It is on the little streams which put into the great valleys the fine sheep-ranches are found. For miles and miles the hills stretch away, covered with a short, soft grass, and on this the sheep keep fat the whole year round. The soil is arid and sandy, and the air warm and dry. All day long the sheep graze on the sweet grass, and at night come down into the valley to drink and sleep. Near Fort Hartsuff, on the head of the North Loup, there is a little valley surrounded by multitudes of low, round hills that look like mounds, and down the valley, over a pebbly bottom, flows a brook of clear, cold water. Near at hand are deep ravines, timber, and cuts in the earth where the hills almost meet overhead. This is a natural sheep-range. The round mounds, of which there are thousands in all directions, are covered with buffalo and gramma grass. The pebbles in the brook clean the sheep's feet, and in winter, when the storms beat, the ravines, timber, and caves give them natural shelter. The snow no sooner falls than the winds blow it off the mounds, and no matter how deep it may be in the valley, by going up two hundred feet the animals can get all the grass they want. There is no need of shelter, for nature has provided corrals for tens of thousands of animals, and it is unnecessary to cut hay, for the grass cured on the ground and always at hand is better than any hay in stacks.

The description of one valley will answer for hundreds of others, as they are very much alike. Lodge Pole Creek, 396 miles west of Omaha, has an elevation of 3861 feet above the level of the sea, and is one of the best ranges in the West for both cattle and sheep. It is 190 miles long, and empties into the South Platte River. For 180 miles it flows adjacent to the Union Pacific Railroad, and the valley in this distance contains at least 1,000,000 acres of grazing-land. The grass is short, sweet, and nutritious, and the range in every way suited to sheep-farming. On the bottoms great quantities of hay could be cut, and in the whole length of Lodge Pole at least 600,000 sheep could be raised, yielding annually 2,500,000 pounds of wool, worth $1,000,000. Horse Creek, 5000 feet above the sea, is located near Cheyenne, Wyoming Territory, and empties into the Platte. It is a fine stream, 100 miles in length, and has Bear Creek, 40 miles long, for a tributary. At the head of Bear Creek is Bear Lake, on the banks of which grow beautiful groves of cotton-wood and box elder. Along the bottom of the main stream is plenty of luxuriant grass for hay, and on the uplands 6,400,000 acres of grazing, where half a million sheep might feed the year round. Larrens Fork is 60 miles long, with hay-lands, uplands, timber, and buffalo grass. Fox Creek is 30 miles long, rises out of solid rock, runs south, and is a fine stock-range. Box Elder is 25 miles long, empties into the Platte, and has plenty of sheep-grass. Deer Creek is 40 miles long and has good pasturage. On both Box Elder and Deer Creek is found aspen, box-elder, and cottonwood timber. Chugwater and its tributaries — Richard Creek, Wolf Creek, Spring Creek, and Willow Creek —are each over 200 miles long, and afford good grazing. Sabille Creek has also good bottoms, and is 40 miles long. The Big Laramie is over 200 miles in length, and has bottoms 5 miles wide. It contains at least 6,400,000 acres of rich grass-lands, on which as many sheep could be grazed, and they would annually produce 24,000,000 pounds of wool, worth $9,600,000. In this one valley of the West could be grazed all the sheep now in the great State of Ohio. As many as 500,000 sheep could be raised each year, and these for mutton alone would be worth $2,500,000. The land on the Laramie Plains is high and dry, and the air pure. There is plenty of timber, and, taken all together, this is a perfect sheep paradise.

All these pasturages are of easy access to the Union Pacific Railroad, and many of them near cities and large towns. The whole country west from Grand Island to Green River, a distance of over five hundred miles, is one vast pasture-field. The Sweetwater Valley, many hundreds of miles long, and from four to ten miles wide, affords rich grass, and would graze 1,000,-000 sheep and cattle. I have been all over the Wind River country, and it is an enormous belt of agricultural and pastoral lands. The valley will grow wheat, rye, oats, Indian corn, and furnish sites for beautiful homes, while on the hills which roll away for hundreds of miles millions of sheep and cattle can graze without other food or shelter than that furnished by nature. Beyond the Wind River is the Big Horn range, of which

General Bradley says : " For stock-raising no country could be finer, and the conditions are such as to insure the minimum of expense and labor and maximum of profits. The fine air and water insure health to the herds and the pasture food all the year round. The country including and bordering on the Big Horn Mountain is particularly fitted for sheep-raising. Sheep like the high land and dry air of such a region, and these, with the fine, rich grasses of the mountain slopes, would produce fleeces not excelled in any part of the world. Sheep-husbandry is as yet in its infancy with us, but the time will come when the Big Horn country will be as famous for its flocks and wool as any part of the old world, perhaps as famous for its looms and mills too."* The climate of these mountains is admirably suited to the culture of goats. The Angora, the finest goat in the world, would grow and thrive here. His fleece would be, too, a valuable addition to our wool market. A Russian traveller, writing of this little animal, says: " His home is on the great mountain slopes, on dry soil, and among feldspathic rocks. His fleece is white as snow, and of dazzling purity, softness, and lustre. The shearing is no sooner concluded than he takes to the mountains, and there, above dew-falling points, he feeds and flourishes on the aromatic plants and dry grasses.

---

* This country was for a long time closed to settlement by Red Cloud's hostile bands, but the Sioux war has opened it up to civilization. Fort Custer is located in the very heart of the Big Horn Valley, and Fort Keogh is only about one hundred miles by land farther down the Yellowstone. The country will ere long be as safe as Nebraska or Colorado.

There is no humidity in this climate; persons who lie out all night in the open air will find in the morning that their garments have not the slightest dampness about them. The goats eat nothing except shoots of vegetation and herbs, and it is this which contributes to make their fleeces so brilliant."

This climate is singularly like our own country along the Big Horn, Wind River, and throughout the Black Hills. Undoubtedly Angora goats would grow and thrive along the whole mountain range of the " Great Rockies."

Some faint idea of the extent and capacity of our immense Western pastoral region may be obtained when we consider that there is grazing-ground enough in Wyoming alone for all the sheep in the United States, Australia, and the Argentine Republic, which now produce an aggregate of 300,000,000 pounds of wool, worth $100,000,000, annually. The United States, with an area of 2,940,000 square miles, produces 100,000,000 pounds of wool, while the British Islands, with an area of only 118,000 square miles, produces 260,000,000 pounds. In other words, with twenty-five times their land, and five hundred times their pasturage, we produce less than one-half as much wool. Buenos Ayres has 75,000,000 head of sheep, and these might be driven into the great West and grazed without occupying one-eighth of our sheep-lands. Between the Missouri River and the Pacific coast there are not less than 1,650,000 square miles of agricultural lands, and more than one billion of acres of grazing lands, capable of grazing conveniently 600,000,000 sheep. It staggers human belief to compute the extent and capacity of our great West, and only those who have ridden over it on horseback, as I have done for twelve years past, can form any idea of its immensity. The valley of the North Platte, from where it joins the South Platte to its mountain source in the north part of Colorado, is 800 miles, making in the whole length 1450 miles of Platte Valley. The two Platte Valleys, with their tributaries, will average 40 miles in width, making 58,000 square miles, equal to 37,000,000 acres. Think of two valleys and their tributaries out West being larger than New York or Pennsylvania! Yet the small portion of New York State devoted to pasturage furnishes grass for 7,000,000 graminivorous animals— horses, sheep, and cattle—valued at $575,000,000. "It is only by comparisons," says Dr. Latham, "the people of the East can form any idea of the capabilities and wealth of the West."

Besides the great Platte Valleys just mentioned are the Loups, Beaver, Shell, Calamus, and Dismal Valleys, which average in the aggregate over 30 miles in width, and have more than 10,000,000 acres of pasture-land along their banks. The temperature in this region for the whole year is 50° Fahrenheit. The mean temperature for spring is 47°, for summer 75°, for autumn 50°, and for winter 25°. The annual rainfall is $25\frac{1}{4}$ inches, divided as follows: spring, 8; summer, 12; autumn, 4; winter (snow, 18 inches), $1\frac{1}{4}$ inches rain.

Dr. Latham, speaking of the country north of Grand Island, on the Union Pacific Railroad, says: "The

Loup Forks and tributaries have 10,000,000 to 12,000,-000 acres of as good.and reliable winter grazing as is to be found in Buenos Ayres, South Africa, or Australia. Wool can be raised as cheaply in this country as anywhere in the world. In other countries they pay land and water transportation of thousands of miles, sell their wool from 12 to 25 cents per pound, and grow rich at that price. On the Loup alone there is room for 7,000,000, and the best grass I have ever seen for graminivorous animals. Ohio has 6,500,000 sheep, which, considered alone for their wool, after pay-𝔵 ing the interest of capital invested in their pasture- and meadow-lands, and the cost of feeding through the six months of winter, do not pay one per cent. on the capital invested in themselves."

These 6,500,000 sheep of Ohio, if they could be transferred to the Platte country, besides making room at home for a paying investment, would pay 25 per cent. profit per annum out West, where the only cost of keeping would be herding.

CHAPTER IX.

GREET PASTURE-LANDS.

Where Sheep can be best Raised—Who the Sheep-Owners of the
Plains are—How the Ranches are managed—Letters from
Sheep-Raisers.

To describe correctly the pasture-lands of the West
would require not one but a dozen chapters, and even
the most important regions can only have a brief mention. The streams flowing into the North Platte on
its north bank alone are the Blue Water, Coldwater,
Slate, Sweetwater, and Sheet.

On the south side are the Ash, Pumpkin, Larrens,
Dry, Horse, Cherry, Chugwater, Sybille, Big Laramie,
Little Laramie, Deer, Medicine, Rock, and Douglas.
These streams with their feeders drain 40,000,000 acres
of pasture-lands; most of them have timber along their
banks, and afford beautiful sites for ranches and residences.

In the North Platte basin, east of the Black Hills,
are 8,000,000 acres of pasturage, with the finest and
most lasting living streams, and good shelter in bluffs
and . cañons. These 8,000,000 acres of pasturage, if
taxed to their capacity, would feed all the year round
8,000,000 head of sheep, yielding 24,000,000 pounds
of wool annually, worth $7,000,000 to $8,000,000.

106

The Republican Valley is 250 miles long, and with its tributaries embraces an area of 25,000 square miles, or 16,000,000 acres of land.

The whole country is divided into plain, bluff, and valley, and there is not a rod of the 16,000,000 acres that is not the finest grazing, and which is not covered with a luxuriant growth of blue, buffalo, and gramma grasses. The whole country is exceptionally well watered by the Republican River, and the great stream has among its tributaries on the north bank Hoickearea, White Man, Black Wood, Eight Mile, Little River, Red, Stinking Water, Medicine, Turkey, and Elm ; on the south bank are Prairie Dog, Sappa Beaver, White, Box Elder, Ash, Cottonwood, and North and South Forks. No particular description of these streams can be given, but they are mostly well timbered, full of beautiful spots and natural homes for hundreds of raisers and tens of thousands of herds. Here the buffalo were thickest, and only ten years ago it was estimated that there were 1,000,000 head grazing on the Republican and its tributaries. They have all gone, and not 50,000 head of cattle or sheep have yet replaced them. What a field for the future stock-kings of the West !

The Cache la Poudre, Big Thompson, St. Vrain, Bijou, Kiawa, Bear, Beaver, Lone Tree, Howard, Crow, Pawnee, Cheyenne, Little Missouri, Cannon Ball, Hart, Belle, Fouche, and many other valleys are famous for their rich grasses, and afford admirable ranges for both cattle and sheep, but to describe these and a hundred other rivers in the great West would require a volume.

I have seen cabbages raised on the Cache la Poudre that weighed fifty pounds each ; turnips, twelve pounds ; potatoes, four pounds ; and beets two feet and a half long. I have also seen cattle in January on the St. Vrain and Big Thompson so fat they could hardly be eaten. At one of our frontier posts is an official record, made in March, complaining of the beef as " too fat for issue to the men," and directing the butcher to select and kill leaner animals. This is the West as a grazing-country ; and if any one doubts let him come and see for himself. He will not only learn the astonishing fact that the natural grasses over-fatten stock, but he can see fields of 10 acres from which 500 bushels of wheat were cut and threshed, and if he will work he can dig 500 bushels of potatoes from a single acre of land.

The increase of the wool-trade has been most marvellous. The wool industry of South America, South Africa, and Australia does not date back more than a quarter of a century, and now they export 250,000,000 pounds.

In England, thirty years ago, there were imported 74,000 bales of wool from Germany, 10,000 bales from Spain and Portugal, 8000 bales from the British colonies, and 5000 bales from other places, making a total of 97,000 bales. In 1864 there were imported from Australia 302,000 bales ; Cape of Good Hope, 68,000 ; South America, 99,000 ; and from all other sources, 219,336 ; in all, 688,336 bales. Australia now supplies more than three times the whole amount of foreign wool consumed in England thirty years ago, and the production of South America exceeds the whole consumption then.

Our own country is not without some remarkable increases, as is shown by Iowa, which had in 1859 258,288 sheep, and in 1879 she had 2,332,241. If the sheep-trade on the Plains increases as rapidly as the cattle-trade has (and there is no apparent reason why it should not), there will soon be in the pasturages along the Union Pacific Railroad alone 1,000,000 head. The cost of bringing sheep to Nebraska, Colorado, Wyoming, and Montana from New Mexico is about $2 per head. Shepherds can be hired at from $30 to $40 per month, and one man can attend about 3000 head. Wool has been carried by railroad from San Francisco to Boston for $1.10 per 100 pounds. Double-decked sheep-cars, carrying 200 sheep, can be had from the base of the mountains to Chicago markets for $150, thereby putting fat wethers in market at 75 cents per head; dressed mutton carcasses are delivered from the Rocky Mountains in New York at $1.75 per hundred, car-load rates.

The principal sheep-owners in the West, with the number of sheep in their herds, are as follows : Moore Brothers, Sydney, Nebraska, 15,000 ; A. M. Munson, Greeley, Colorado, 5000 ; Mr. Bailey, South Platte, 3000 ; Hutton, Alsop & Creighton, Laramie, Wyoming, 13,000 ; Carters & Co., Plains, 3000 ; J. W. H. Iliff, Colorado, 10,000 ; Amigo Brothers, Colorado, 50,000 ; Hollester & Co., Utah, 20,000 ; Willard Clark & Co., Laramie Plains, 3000 ; Rumsey & Co., Laramie Plains, 2000 ; E. M. Post, Cheyenne, 5000 ; Ballentine Brothers, Nebraska, 5000; Maxwell Estate, Colorado, 20,000 ; Benito Bacco, Colorado, 40,000; J. S. Maynard, Colorado, 5000 ; A. M. Merriman, Colorado, 3000 ; Patterson Brothers, Colorado, 20,000 ; Keith & Co., Nebraska, 2000 ; Dr. A. W. Bell, Colorado, 1000 ; George Burk, Nebraska, 1000 ; Froman Brothers, Nebraska, 1000 ; Alfred Way, Nebraska, 1200 ; Alfaugh & Grover, Nebraska, 1500 ; Andy Struthers, Nebraska, 1000 ; H. Coolidge, Nebraska, 300 ; A. Stuart, Nebraska, 400 ; Coe, Carter & Bratt, Nebraska, 900 ; Theodore Bye, Nebraska, 200 ; C. Mylander, Nebraska, 200 ; King & Lane, Laramie, Wyoming, 2000.

There are many large sheep-herds in New Mexico and Texas, but as these could hardly be called Western herds they are omitted from this chapter. The Amigo Brothers alone own in the Southwest over 300,000 sheep.

Referring particularly to some of the herds above enumerated, I may mention that of Willard Clark & Co. It is located eighteen miles from Laramie City, Wyoming Territory, on the Laramie Plains, and about six miles from the base of the mountains. The soil is coarse, gravelly, and formed of *débris* washed from the mountain-side. The whole Laramie Plain resembles the bottom of an old lake, and the basin, seventy miles long, was no doubt once covered with water.

Near the mountains the streams are small, clear, and cold, being fed by melted snows, but in the valley, where they are larger, they frequently overflow and deposit a rich, alluvial soil along their banks. In the

Plain the grass is rank and rich, and on the slopes the soil is sandy and herbage sparse. It is on these barren uplands the sheep love to dwell, and where they seem to thrive best, while the flat-lands are reserved for cattle-ranges. The atmosphere is very clear, and objects ten miles off do not appear to be over two miles distant. It would be impossible for any one to take a pulmonary disease in such a climate, and it would be a very bad case of consumption, indeed, which could not be cured by a year's sheep-herding on the Plains. Every one sleeps out in the open air at night, and although the thermometer often drops down below zero there is not the slightest danger of taking cold or contracting rheumatism.

Mr. Edward Curly, of the London *Field*, speaking of the climate of these Plains, says: "Snow will gradually disappear while the temperature is constantly below freezing-point. Place a saucer of anhydrous sulphuric acid under a glass bell, with a little snow around it, on a very cold day, and you can produce the same effect on a very small scale in England, and from the same cause. The boiled acid will make the air within the glass so very dry that it will drink up the snow, or cause it to evaporate without going through the intermediate process of melting. Moisten a piece of cambric and hang it out in the wind on the Plains on a very cold day, and it will freeze quite stiff immediately, and in a short time be quite dry and limp. The ice within the fibrous threads has evaporated without melting, precisely as the snows of Wyoming or Colorado waste away."

Mr. Clark has a substantial house, stables for horses, and sheds for 4000 sheep. He keeps hay for his sheep, and in so high a latitude such a precaution is certainly necessary. A mile and a half above the sea, he lives as warm and comfortable in winter as the people of New York, and never knows what it is to suffer with heat in summer. The following is a statement of a portion of Mr. Clark's operations in sheep:

First Year.

Cost of ranch and implements	$4,350
300 tons of hay two seasons	650
May, 1879, bought 140 merino sheep, of which 18 were full-grown rams, and 3 ram lambs. Average net cost for the lot	2,100
August, 1879, bought 2000 native ewes, at $3 each .	6,000
Total	$12,100

Returns: Shearing of 1880, 9200 pounds wool; net 29 cents per pound	$2,668
Value of 25 pure-blood merino ram lambs, at $25 each .	1,125
Value 1515 common-blood lambs, at an average of $3 each	4,545
Total	$8,338

The data is too imperfect to fix a ratio of profits, but Mr. Clark said in another year he would have his herd and establishment clear, and if in three years one can clear a herd and ranch worth $12,000, he would, I think, be doing very well.

Mr. H. B. Rumsey has a flock on the Laramie Plains, and the following is a return of his first three years of sheep-growing out West:

First Year.

Bought 650 ewes, at a cost of $3 each	$1950
" 1 ranch, with sheds	1200
40 tons of hay, at $6 per ton	240
Team, wagon, etc.	200
Two horses for herding	100
Total	$3690

Expenses: Labor for one year	$600
Board foreman one year	100
Horse-feed	100
Shearing sheep	50
Incidentals	100
Total	$950

Returns: Sold 3600 pounds wool, at 29 cents per pound	$1044
On hand, 420 lambs, for which had an offer of $4.50, but say $3 each	1260
Total	$2304
Deduct expenses	950
Net profit, equal to about 35 per cent.	$1354

Mr. Rumsey, in his estimate for next year, stated:

1500 sheep, extra sheds, horses, wagons, fencing, hay, improvements, labor on ranches, etc., total about		$8000
Returns of wool from 1500 sheep, five pounds to the fleece, 7500 pounds, at 25 cents per pound . .		1875
Increase, 70 per cent., 1050 lambs, at $3 each . . .		3150
Total		$5025
Expenses: Labor for one year . . .	$800	
Contingent fund	500	
		1300
Net profit (exclusive of improved value of sheep, 46½ per cent. on investment)		$3725

The greatest possible difference of opinion exists among sheep-owners as to the proper manner of breeding. Some breed in, and others out; some say sheep should be bred up to the highest point, while others contend a cross is best. Without pretending to express an opinion, I would, if handling a herd, breed up Cotswolds for mutton, and cross merinos with Cotswolds for wool. A great many owners say the French merino is greatly to be preferred to the Spanish merino for breeding in this country. The Cotswold cross with the merino gives a large-bodied sheep, and a good quality of wool. The cross between the Mexican sheep and merino does not materially increase the size of the sheep, but the wool is good. A lot of Mexican ewes can be had at Denver, Cheyenne, or Pueblo for $2 per head, but they are valuable only for starting a herd. These ewes are very prolific, but they are small, their wool coarse, and of little value. A well-known authority on breeding says: " While I fully concur in the desirableness of the cross between the merinos and Cotswolds for hardihood, large fleeces, and good mutton, I will say that the Leicesters are to my view very similar to the Cotswolds, and what is claimed for the latter in the cross referred to may be equally claimed for the former." The large bodies, good health, fine mutton, rather than wool, is the principal recommendation of the cross between merinos and Cotswolds. To breed up a herd rapidly for profit take the largest Mexican ewes and best Cotswold rams.

Mr. Merriman, who has his herd about six miles from Colorado Springs, says: " At present I have about 3000 head of sheep, a cross between the Mexican ewes and the merinos, about two-thirds of the herd being ewes. The cost of these is $2 each, and of the merino bucks $30 each. I keep two bucks to every hundred ewes. My average clip is three pounds per head a year, and I estimate the value of the clip at 35 to 40 cents per pound. It required one man only to herd the flock, and I pay him $45 per month, including board. The bucks I keep in an enclosed pasture, commencing May 1st and to be continued to December 1st of each year. I divide my herd, putting the breeding ewes in a separate flock from the wethers and lambs, requiring two herders, one for each flock; but I think it pays to incur the additional expense, and I shall keep it up in the future. My average increase is about 75 per cent. for the ewes, or 50 per cent. for the whole flock per annum. In five years' experience I have never fed any hay or grain to my flock, and depend entirely on the native grasses, with a few exceptions, as in cases of sickness, or some fine-blooded bucks or ewes. I think we can claim in Colorado to be entirely exempt from disease incident to sheep in the States, such as foot-rot and scab. I have never had the least trouble with them here." Mr. Merriman is a careful breeder, has succeeded well, and his experience is very instructive and interesting.

On the Laramie Plains considerable trouble was had with scab, but a complete antidote and cure was found in tobacco dip. A few pounds of tobacco boiled and the juice mixed with water will dip many sheep, and a souse each spring after shearing will keep them clear of scab. When large herds have to be dipped, a tank ten feet square and two and a half feet deep, filled with tobacco-dip, is put at the mouth of the corral, and the sheep driven through it. A jump in and a jump out is all they need for the year in order to ensure complete health. If, however, I were going into sheep-growing out West, I would not go so far north as the Laramie Plains, but keep farther south, where the climate is warmer.

Dr. A. W. Bell, who lives at Colorado Springs, has about 1500 sheep, which he keeps nine miles north of that place. His average yield of wool was four and a half pounds per head, and brought in Denver 35 cents and 40 cents per pound. Off 1000 sheep he cut $2500 worth of wool, being about twice the cost of herding and keeping. The increase of the flock was 50 per cent., which, added to his sale of wool, gave him over expenses an income of 60 to 65 per cent. on his investment. Sheep are said to be most remarkably prolific in Colorado, and more twins and triplets are born in that State than anywhere else in the West.

Mexican sheep are very cheap in Colorado, and have been bought as low as 75 cents per head, but the recent demand for stock-sheep in the northern part of the State, and the increased facilities for shipping wool, have sent the price up, and I doubt now if they can be bought for a much less rate than $1.50 and $2 per head. Mexican sheep crossed with merino are worth $2 and $2.50, and good graded sheep bred up bring $5 and $6 each. Blooded bucks are worth from $30 to $200 apiece.

General Cameron, writing of the stock-grasses of

Colorado, says : "Botanists, I believe, make out over fifty varieties of grasses in Colorado alone. Some of these so closely resemble each other as to be regarded by the unscientific as one and the same. Not every person growing stock in Colorado can with certainty tell the difference between gramma grass, buffalo grass, buchloë dactyloides, or sheep fescue (*festuca ovina*). They are generally confounded under one name, as gramma or buffalo grass, and while to the scientific they vary, they are described by the practical herdsman as one. They are the great grasses of the Plains, and constitute the bulk of the winter pasture. When not artificially irrigated they grow on the uplands from one and a half to two and a half inches high, less rather than more, having a dark-green leaf, inclining to curl, the buffalo more than the true gramma. When ripened by the June sun they assume a brown color rather than a straw- or yellow, and give a sombre aspect to the great Plains. When the new growth commences in the spring it is not by new shoots but an elongation of the old ones, carrying the brown hay of the former years on the end of its green leaf. The gramma grasses do not grow tall or produce seed unless irrigated, when they seed at about twelve to sixteen inches in height, making most excellent hay. There is only one other herd-grass deserving especial mention, it is the bunch-grass (*festuca duriuscula*). There are many grasses growing in bunches, but this is the one known by that name, and a great favorite to the herdsman as well as to the cattle, both from its nutritious quality and from the fact of its standing taller

-and stronger than the other grasses, and thus reaching above the snow after a severe storm. It grows upon the hills and in many places on the mountains, and on the divide, but it is very difficult to find far out upon the open plains; it grows with a stem at least a foot high, and after the summer cure has a light-yellow leaf, tinged with red. The bottom-land or hay-grasses are altogether different from those of the upland plains, and consist chiefly of a large leaf marsh grass, differing from that of Illinois and Indiana by having a smooth instead of a serrated edge; also a sweet stem, colored blue, and with a red top. These prairie-grasses, always looking dry and brown, strike the eye of the farmer from the New England States very unfavorably. But short, velvety, and brown as they are they are no doubt the richest in the world, as they not only carry cattle and sheep through the winter fit for beef (the markets of Colorado never saw stall-fed beef), but actually advance the grade of all stock fed upon them."

General Cameron is no doubt correct in all he says about Colorado grasses, but I have seen gramma six inches high in the Powder River country, and loaded with seed on perfectly dry plains. The buffalo grass there is also five and six inches high, and so soft and dry it might be used for stuffing cushions.

CHAPTER X.

A SHEEP RANCH.

What kind of a Ranch to Select—Profits of Sheep-Growing—
Mr. Post's Herd—Letters from Hon. Wm. D. Kelley, Senator
Conkling, and Hon. J. B. Grinnell.

THE three conditions of a good sheep-ranch are
wood, water, and grass. A high, rolling land for
grazing, a flat for hay, to be used in case of emergency,
and deep wooded ravines for shelter from storms. The
streams, if possible, should be living all the year round,
with pebbly bottoms, to cleanse the sheep's hoofs and
prevent foot-rot. Herding is the chief expense in
sheep-raising. A good herder can get $30, $40, and
$50 per month, with food, lodging, and ponies.
These are the highest rates paid, and greatly increased
by the newness of the country. There are few females
out West, and the men have to do their own house-
keeping and cooking, which takes up much of their
time. The minimum of expense is only reached when
a man with a family raises sheep,—the wife and girls
keep house, and the boys and their father do the
herding. The climate is favorable for open and pastoral life, and for eight months in the year there is no
reason why the family, with their tents, could not follow the herd and live perfectly comfortable. The time

will come when we will have both shepherds and shepherdesses on the Plains, and when the patriarch, as of old, with his sons, daughters, and sons' wives and daughters, will follow the herds, crook in hand. Any large family can become rich by following the herds,— the mother caring for the home, and the children, as soon as they are able to ride, being set to mind the flocks. With $500 or $1000 in hand a suitable herd can be started and ranch provided. Of course he would have to build his own house for the winter, with stables and corrals for animals, but this any one can do. In sheep-shearing time, unless an expert at the business, he would have to hire a shearer at eight cents per fleece; but now, since the bands of shearers from New Mexico and Colorado come North, a fleece can be cut for five cents, and, in some instances, three cents. The shearers are a strange set, and every year are becoming more numerous. They cut a fleece with marvellous rapidity, and want little else than their food and clothing, with sometimes a pipe and glass of beverage after supper. They stroll in bands, hunting sheep to shear, and there appears to be a strange fascination about such a nomadic life. Sheep-shearing is now a regular business in the Southwest, and there are now men who do little else for a living. The young sheep-grower would have to lay out of his money about eight months from the time of buying his herd; then the wool-clip would provide him with sufficient funds for all his wants until another clip came in. He need not, unless he desires it, sell any of his sheep, but live off the proceeds of his wool, and allow the herd to increase.

Mr. Curley says: "Suppose an Englishman were to come over to America and go to sheep-raising? He should bring £500 in hand, which, if judiciously handled, would enable him to start with 500 native ewes, perhaps more, with ponies, house, mowing-machine, wagon, rake, and a few household necessaries. He should retain £50 in hand for contingent expenses. His wool the first year would bring him from £80 to £90,—enough to provide contingent expenses for the next year,—and his increase of lambs would certainly be 350, worth £200. The next year the wool would probably bring him from £60 to £75 over and above his expenses. The increase, about 425 lambs, would be worth £225, making £300 profit. This year he would sell 175 wethers, and add at least 200 ewes, with a few thoroughbreds and a proper proportion of bucks to his flock. He would then have about 875 ewes, 225 ewe-lambs, and 225 wether-lambs; or, including the bucks, upwards of 1350 sheep. The wool would bring him £150 to £200 over his expenses, and the increase of 600 to 650 lambs would be worth about £375, making his profit £525 to £575 for the year. His establishment would now be worth at least £1300, and if his sheep were superior in quality, and his improvements the result of much well-directed labor, they might very probably bring £2000. From this time he would have to hire assistance, unless his boys were old enough to herd; but his gains would be exceedingly rapid, and he might reasonably expect to retire with a fortune in a few years." If one were to commence with 200 or 400 ewes the expense would be about the same and the increase slower, so it is important that the grower should have as many ewes as possible with which to begin business.

Mr. E. M. Post, of Cheyenne, Wyoming Territory, is quite an extensive sheep-grower. His herd is made up of Mexican sheep which he is crossing with merinos; the mutton is excellent, but the wool poor and coarse. The ewes breed with wonderful rapidity, and in lambing time four men are employed to look after the little ones until they get strong enough to take care of themselves. Mr. Post thinks it is economy to hire plenty of help during the dropping season. Eight men are required in shearing time, and the average yield is about three pounds to the fleece, worth 25 cents per pound. The cross-breeds shear the first year three pounds each, but of a much better quality of wool, and second year four to five pounds. Mr. Post's account for his herd for a year stood as follows:

3200 Mexican sheep, bought at $2 per head . . .	$6400
Corrals and hay	1500
Merino bucks, $50 each, one to every 100 ewes, 2000 ewes	1000
Total	$8900

Expenses, labor, and incidentals	$1000
Losses, 2 per cent.	128
Total	$1128

Returns: Wool, 9000 pounds, at 25 cents per pound .	$2250
Increase from 2000 ewes, 1800 lambs, at $2.25 each .	4050
Total	$6300
Deduct expenses	1128
Net profit, or 60 per cent. on investment . . .	$5172

The comparative cost of keeping sheep in the United States and on the Plains is stated as follows :

3000 sheep in States, at $2.65 per head . . .		$7950
3000 sheep on the Plains; one herder at $50 per month, including board.	$600	
150 tons of hay, to be used in case of severe winters and storms, at $4 per ton	600	
Total	———	1200
Difference in favor of the Plains		$6750

Under ordinary circumstances the hay could be kept over, and one cutting might do for two or three years.

Having now given my own version of sheep-growing out West, and expressed fully my opinion as to the capabilities and value of our national sheep-walks, I will give the opinions of eminent men and experienced herders who have experimented and studied sheep-culture as connected with the resources of the trans-Missouri country.

Judge Kingman, of Wyoming, who, for the past eight years, has owned sheep-herds, writes as follows: "It will be remembered that the natural habitat of the sheep, as well as of the goat and the antelope, is an elevated, mountainous region. They are provided with an external covering and a constitutional system fitting them to endure its rigors and subsist on its peculiar herbage. They may be removed to other regions, it is true, and by careful husbandry made to flourish in hot climates on artificial or cultivated food, and even in rainy and muddy localities. But the multiplied diseases to which they are subjected are convincing proofs

that they are exposed to influences unnatural and un-
congenial to their constitution. They require a dry,
gravelly soil; a clear, bracing, cool atmosphere; a
variety of short, nutritious grasses; and they love to
browse on highly aromatic plants and shrubs, like the
willow, the birch, the hemlock, and the artemisia. In
such circumstances they are always healthy, vigorous,
and active, and produce the maximum of even-fibred
wool and the best of high-flavored meat. That we have
millions of acres answering in all respects to the exact
requirements for the best development of sheep in the
production of both wool and meat, is demonstrated by
the countless numbers of antelope that annually swarm
over the country, and seem to have no limit to their
increase but their natural enemies, the wolves and the
hunters.

"They are always in good condition, healthy, fat, and
active, and this is particularly noticeable in the winter
and spring, when it might be supposed they would be
reduced by cold and want of food. It is well understood by wool-growers that the great difficulty in producing a staple of uniform evenness and uniform curve
is the variable condition of the sheep at different seasons of the year. The animal organization cannot produce the same quality of growth in extreme cold
weather on dry hay that it will produce in warm
weather on fresh grass. The result is that the best
quality of wool cannot be grown where the sheep are
exposed to extremes of climate, and particularly where
they cannot be kept in uniform good health and condition. If this is true in the growth of wool, it needs

no argument to prove that it is also true in the production of wholesome and nutritious meat. A generous diet of rich and various food is required to keep up a rapid and constant growth, and it is quick growth, combined with good health, that makes the choicest meat. I have been familiar with sheep-raising in New England for many years, and although sheep do pretty well on the rocky hills there, yet they are subject to a frightfully long list of diseases, every one of which, however, is ascribed to local and not inherent causes. The one great cause, exceeding all others in the variety and extent of its evils, is the long-continued rainy weather. The ground gets saturated with water, the feet become soft and tender with the soaking, and foot-disease is propagated by inoculation with surprising rapidity. The fleece gets wet, and remaining so for several days, keeps the animal enveloped in a steam-bath; this produces pustules, scab, tetter, and other cutaneous diseases. Every thing and every place is soaked and dripping with water during those long storms, and the sheep are compelled to lie on the wet ground, and contract colic, scours, stretchers, and other bowel diseases. But here, on our hard, porous, gravelly soil, in a bright, equable climate, a dry, bracing atmosphere, having abundance of nutritious grasses and a great variety of desirable food, the flocks will find every circumstance contributing to their perfect growth and development. This is such a country and climate as they naturally inhabit. Their constitutions are fitted to its peculiarities, and will produce here their highest possibilities. There is no doubt that any breed of sheep will do well here, but for various reasons I would advise the introduction of the best qualities of mutton-sheep in preference to the fine-wooled animals. In the first place, they are hardier and more prolific, and will undoubtedly improve faster; in the second place, while it is possible to overstock the market with wool by importation from foreign countries, it is not possible to overstock the meat market. We have now 47,000,000 of people, and the annual increase is about 3,000,000; our people are all meat eaters; the price of meat in our large cities is enormously high, and the annual production by no means keeps pace with the demand for consumption. But, in addition to all this, the actual return in wool from a flock of medium-wooled sheep will nearly equal in value the net product of a fine-wooled flock. They produce heavier fleeces, and the price of the wool bears a better ratio to its cost. Most of our flock-masters are purchasing the sheep-flocks of New Mexico and the extreme Western States, with the expectation of getting good animals by crossing. This may be done, it is true, but I do not think it likely to result satisfactorily. It requires too much care and judicious selection, as well as long-continued effort, to get rid of bad qualities and fix permanently good ones. We can get sheep, by going farther East, which have been carefully improved for fifty years, and in which the characteristics have been developed by a scientific breeding which we may not hope to equal. Such a flock will cost more to start with, and will be worth more, but may not have cost more, all things considered, after a few years."

Hon. J. Francisco Chaves, of New Mexico, writes : " Without having the data before me, and only judging from what I know of the Territory and of the large sheep-owners in it, I am satisfied that I do not overestimate the number in stating them at 1,500,000 head of ewes. The climate is extremely temperate and salubrious, no diseases, much less those affecting the skin or hoofs, being known. Sheep in our Territory are herded and grazed from one portion of the Territory to another during the same year, thus adopting what may be termed the migratory plan. The climate is dry and the soil is gravelly, producing the most nutritious grasses and shrubs. Of the former the gramma and bunch grass, of which there are two or three different varieties, and the latter, the various kinds of sage, which make the best and most nutritious of browsing, and a large amount of underbrush and seed-grass in the mountains. Were it not for the insecurity of life and property caused by the wild marauding tribes of Indians, especially the Navajoes, but a few years would elapse before New Mexico's hills and plains would be literally covered with fleecy flocks. It is but a few years back, and actually within my own personal recollection, when nearly 1,000,000 of sheep were annually driven to market to Southern Mexico from our Territory. At that time sheep were worth but 25 cents per head, and all those engaged in the business made money. That prosperity in the history of New Mexico was superinduced by twelve years of unintermitted peace with the Navajoes. A sheep-raiser in New Mexico can safely calculate on an increase of 80 per centum at least. A sheep-raiser in New Mexico, notwithstanding the coarse quality of wool of the present flock, can herd his sheep and make a profit from the product of his wool, and have all the increase of his stock in addition thereto. I have no hesitation in saying that New Mexico can fairly compete with Australia, South Africa, and South America in the production of cheap wool. These statements may appear to you somewhat exaggerated, but I assure you, on the contrary, that it is within the limits of reasonable bounds. I was born and raised in New Mexico, my friends and relations have always owned sheep, and I myself have to a large extent been an owner of that kind of property, and, therefore, to a great extent speak from personal experience."

Senator Chaffee, of Colorado, says: " In one county (Conejoes) out of the twenty-one counties of Colorado over 300,000 sheep were grazing at one time last summer, and I do not think 1,500,000 would be an overestimate for the whole Territory. The character of the climate and soil being dry (the latter being also gravelly and porous) the grasses are very nutritious, with a great variety of food in the great variety of aromatic plants of that country, renders them scarcely liable to disease. It is undoubtedly the most natural and finely-adapted sheep-growing country in the world, and I think this is the universal testimony of those best acquainted with stock-raising who have visited Colorado in the last few years. In the southern portion of Colorado the only cost is herding, and, subsisting upon the natural grasses of the country in winter as well as summer, no preparations of hay or other food are necessary. The net profit is reckoned, after deducting every expense, at not less than 40 per cent., and by others at 75 per cent., per annum upon the investment, and this is at the present low prices, and for our inferior grades of wool. Woollen-manufactories are springing up in that country, which will increase the price of wool by creating a better market, and at no distant day will that country be the most extensive woollen-manufacturing country of this continent. The eastern slope of the Rocky Mountains, including Wyoming, Colorado, and New Mexico, is doubtless the best sheep-growing region on this continent, and likely of the world, and is capable of grazing more sheep and cheaper than all the rest of the United States together."

Hon. W. H. Hooper, of Utah, writes : " The climate, grasses, and topography of that country render it one of the best sheep-producing localities in the whole range of States and Territories, and I claim that in this respect what I say for Utah will almost wholly apply to the entire Rocky Mountain country. The sheep are healthy and prolific, and afford the finest mutton I have ever eaten, and their fleeces are in quantity and quality all that could be desired. The people of my Territory have from necessity given to the subject of sheep-growing as full and careful a test, if not more so, than any other settling the higher regions of the far West. Their destitute condition on arriving at Salt Lake compelled them to give early and thorough attention to home productions, as their fine flocks of sheep and their numerous woollen- and cotton-factories which followed their settlement of that country will attest. I think there are now running in Utah five woollen-factories, which are far behind in working up the wool produced. Other factories are now being built, one of them designed for three thousand spindles, which will manufacture different and finer cloths than any now made in our Territory. I am entirely satisfied that we shall be able not only to clothe our present population with these home products, making these investments at the same time profitable and self-sustaining, but be able to provide for the large influx that yearly is adding to our numbers. And we are pleased to know that with these additions are many skilled workmen in the woollens, as well as other branches of mechanism. One very advantageous feature of the Rocky Mountain range in sheep-growing is the adaptability of our many valleys for the raising of roots, which afford them good food and enables their owners—those in the higher and more northern and more snowy portions—to feed them well, and thus render more certain a large number of lambs and a larger yield of wool. So much for our sheep. Let me tell you, also, that Utah has cotton-factories, and grows the upland cotton to run them ; and though it may not in the cent per cent view be a big-paying interest, still it helps to render the people to a great degree independent. Madder and indigo are produced in Southern Utah enough for domestic use. Let me also say that our vineyards, so productive, will soon enable us to furnish wine for export. The other fruits you know are thrifty and prolific, and no finer flavored fruit is grown anywhere. Silk-growing, too, is soon to be one of our great interests, experiments in that dircetion having proved very successful. Indeed, I may safely say that next to wool-growing silk-growing will soon take the place for utility and profit. The mulberry-tree grows luxuriantly under the care of the husbandman, and as a shade-tree it is incomparable for beauty. We are doing much to prepare the way to add this industry, of so much interest to the whole world, to the numerous and growing interests to which Utah can to-day point with so much pride."

Hon. S. F. Nuckolls, of Wyoming, a member of Congress (now deceased), wrote : " I would say briefly that the soil, grasses, and climate render it eminently superior, especially for sheep. The soil absorbs the falling rain rapidly, while its lighter particles refuse to attach permanently to the fleece, affording a clip as clean without washing as in other countries with washing. The grasses are highly nutritious, cure on the ground, remain as permanent food during the entire winter, and have better fattening properties than the prairie-grasses in the more eastern and northern States. The position is elevated, the air pure, and the ground seldom muddy or soft. In addition to all this there are no burrs of any kind, which are such pests in other regions. Sheep are, therefore, healthy and free from foot-rot and other distempers common to low, moist lands and rank, coarse food. They have been kept for the past twelve years about the military posts without trouble, and last winter some 30,000 went through without shelter or food other than the grass on the ground. The flocks of James A. Moore & Brother, near Cheyenne, composed of common merino and small

Mexican sheep, averaged five pounds to the fleece. Cattle in large quantities are kept in the same way, and the cattle worked poor in freighting turned out in fall are fat and ready for the yoke or the butcher when spring comes. The quantity of lands adapted to this business along the eastern slope, in the valleys and mountains, is simply immense, amounting to millions of acres. The facilities for sale and shipment are all that can be asked or needed. I have no hesitation in saying that these lands are destined to supply the wool and mutton for a large part of the country, and preserve this industry now being driven out of the Eastern and Northern States by the cost of winter feed and the greater value of lands for other purposes. I may also add that the snow never falls to any great depth on the grazing-lands, and is taken up by the atmosphere, often leaving scarcely a trace of dampness on the ground."

Governor Thayer, of Wyoming, writes: "In some respects I look upon grazing as the most important of the varied resources of that region. It is the most important, as the great want of our population is a plentiful supply of cheap animal food. It is also important as the only means of furnishing cheap wool from which to manufacture low-priced clothing for our laboring classes and for exportation. The interior of all continents, with their high, dry, and comparatively arid table-lands, has furnished winter grazing, by which means low-priced wool has been grown. It is so with Asia, Africa, and South America and Australia. It will be pre-eminently so with all that country west of the Missouri River. The experience of the freighters on the Plains and in the mountains for a quarter of a century leaves no doubt of the certainty of winter grazing for horses, sheep, and cattle in that greater half of our country. I am sure that wool can be grown there equal in fibre to the best wools of Australia, Saxony, Silesia, or Moravia, or at as low prices as any wool can be grown on the cheapest pastures of the world, and still leave a wide margin to the flock-masters for profit. We ought to grow all the wool there not only for our own wants but for the use of the non-wool-growing world. When we grow the necessary fibres I have no doubt we shall then be able to produce cheap and fine fabrics at prices that will enable us to compete in the markets of the world with those of any country. The overshadowing importance of this subject should attract the attention of every economist in the country."

Hon. W. D. Kelley, of Pennsylvania, who has spent much time on the Plains, says of them : "Two industries, each of primary importance to the country, should be introduced at an early day, because both will find there the conditions under which they may be brought almost immediately to absolute perfection. I mean the growth of wool, both from the Angora and Cashmere goats and the sheep, and the production of the best beet-root sugar. For the latter, Grant, in his admirable little book, says the primary essentials are cheap land and fuel and pure water. All these you have wherever the melting snow of the mountains can be carried for irrigation, and in the neighborhood of your mountain streams. Your natural grasses and aromatic herbage are identical with those of the great sheep-fields

of Asia and Australia; and should you establish the
production of the beet and the manufacture of sugar on
a large scale, you will find, as it has been found everywhere else, that three tons of the refuse beet, from
which the saccharine matter has been expressed, will
be equivalent to two tons of the best hay in sustaining
and fattening sheep and cattle. It therefore seems to
me that you will render a very important service, not
only to your own section but to the country at large,
if by making known these peculiar resources you pro-
mote the establishment of two such vital industries.
Either of them will doubtless succeed if undertaken
by proper hands; but both should be established, as
each will contribute to the success of the other."

Senator Conkling, of New York, writes: "On all
occasions of traversing the Plains—and I have crossed
them several times—my attention has been attracted to
the adaptation of the country to flocks. Indeed, the
most broken, abrupt, and waste places seemed to me
available for sheep-grazing. The dryness and softness
of the ground is one of the elements in the case to be
noticed; but I am writing too hastily to do more than
bear testimony to the conclusion to which I came."

Hon. William Lawrence, of Ohio, an extensive
sheep-raiser, writes of the Plains: "I have been and
am somewhat interested in raising sheep and producing
wool in Ohio, and I have given some attention to the
subject. I expressed my opinion of the future of
sheep-husbandry in this country in a speech which I
made, April 8, 1878, in Congress, and which I yet
believe to be correct. I then expressed the opinion

that the interior of this country would in a few years produce nearly all the wool that would be required in the United States for our home supply, and in fact I do not entertain any doubt but that in twenty years enough wool can be raised to supply not only the home demand but enough for all the export trade this country can command. I have passed over the railroad from Omaha to San Francisco. I stopped at Laramie, in Wyoming Territory. There I saw a herd of 4000 cattle and some 3000 sheep grazing in Laramie Valley in healthy condition and good order. Laramie Valley is about one hundred miles long and thirty miles wide, as I there learned, covered mainly with a short but very nutritious grass well adapted to grazing cattle and sheep. The climate, as I learned, was generally cool, with a healthful, bracing atmosphere, with nothing to produce disease either in man or stock. I mention this valley because I examined it more carefully than any other, but from what I saw and learned I am satisfied a large part of the great central interior of this continent is of the same description of land. I cannot doubt that this in a few years will become the principal stock-raising portion of our country. Sheep can be raised at no expense except herding, and, in some places, the cost of cutting enough grass along the streams for hay to feed a short time in the winter, while in much of this vast region, as I learn, sheep can be kept the year round in good order without hay or grain, simply by grazing. I cannot doubt but in a few years wool will be produced so cheap and in such quantities that it cannot be imported from abroad. When our home supply of wool shall thus be increased, and rendered as cheap or cheaper than wool can be imported, I cannot see why this will not become the greatest manufacturing country in the world, and a vast supply of cheap agricultural products. Woollen-manufactories must spring up in great abundance, and the United States will become exporters instead of importers of woollen goods. One result of this will be that a new and vastly increased market will be created for the agricultural products of the grain-growing States. The soil and climate are not adapted to grain-growing, unless by irrigation, west of the central portion of Kansas and Nebraska; hence the production of wool in the trans-Missouri country will create a demand for agricultural products there, and manufactories will multiply to still increase the demand. Already the prospect of sheep-growing in this interior region is having its effects. In two years the sheep of Ohio have diminished 2,579,-410 in numbers, in part, doubtless, owing to the considerations I have named. It is, in my judgment, only a question of time, and that a few years at most, when sheep-growing for wool will be transferred to this great central region. These are the opinions I entertain, and if they can be of any service in assisting you to attract the attention of our Eastern people to this undeveloped resource of that greater half of our country, I shall proudly feel that I have contributed a very little to aid in developing a vast region of country, and in opening it up as a source of untold wealth. With the vast product of wool that is soon to come from this great interior region, I believe, too, there will soon spring up in various portions of the United States the grandest and most extensive manufacturing enterprises the world has ever seen. All questions of free trade will be settled in a few years by these interior sources of wealth."

In an able, exhaustive article on "Sheep on the Prairies," the Hon. J. B. Grinnell, of Iowa, in speaking of the necessity of a varied agriculture, says: "The States of Missouri, Iowa, Kansas, Illinois, Minnesota, Wisconsin, and Michigan have expended more than $200,000,000 in the construction of railroads. They have brought life to a thousand cities and villages on the 'iron ways,' and wealth to such farmers as have found a near market and an easy transportation of their grain to the older States. But the demand for grain is met, the warehouses are full, and in the Northwest wheat is a drug, and the future is not full of promise to the grain-raiser. Our lands are fast being exhausted, and for a wheat market we must depend upon a scarcity in the Old World, and even then the profits must be determined by the carriers and toll-gatherers of sea and land, who fix their rates of transportation as high as possible and yet not amount to a prohibition of the products raised for market. Wool is no exotic. Earnestness and skill are the first requisites, and a production of wool equal to all the wants of the dwellers on the continent will be at hand, bringing into us millions of acres of the finest native sheep-walks, now producing grass that is just suited to the flock. Disturbed labor and an inadequate production point to a virgin empire in extent, and invite the world

to a way of wealth, which secured, diversifies our
productions, gives scope to national enterprise, subsistence and hope to those who would find a homestead
on the free lands of the West. At any point two hundred miles from Chicago this ratio of freight is well
established: That to transport your products to the
seaboard, on wheat you pay 80 per cent. of its value;
on pork, 30 per cent.; on beef, 20 per cent.; on wool,
4 per cent. This is no conjecture, but my own experience, that I give 80 per cent. of the value of wheat,
which impoverishes my farm, to find a market for it,
and 4 per cent. to find the best wool-market, the production of which enriches my acres beyond calculation.
National development and expansion are involved in
the early clothing of our prairies with bleating flocks.
We have room and occupation for hundreds of thousands who should go forth from our teeming cities to
escape crowded garrets and death-damp of cellars. To
the young man who believes 'the behavior of sheep as
fascinating under any circumstances,' and finds no room
on the old-farm in the East, we can say: Here is room,
an unclaimed area, larger by thousands of square miles
than the land of Midian, from which the Israelites
brought forth 750,000 sheep as spoils,—a range of
country from Southern Kansas on the south to St. Paul
on the north, as varied in climate and production, and
better adapted to the wants of the shepherd than the
famed walks of Spain,—varying as the southern plains
of Andalusia and the northern snow-clad mountains,
on and between which extremes there were depastured
with profit several millions of sheep, the progenitors of

our famed merinos. Our national sheep-walks, as yet untrod by the golden hoof, embrace an area of country larger than the pastures of ancient Assyria and the famed pastures of Europe, and had we a population one-half as dense as the sheep-districts of France and Spain, without lessening the other staple products sent to market, we could clothe our own people, and produce a sufficiency of wool at 40 cents per pound to pay interest and principal on our debt of $2,000,000,000 within the time which has been required to earn the well-deserved name of our American merinos."

I can bear testimony to the entire truth of what Mr. Grinnell says. In one flock of over 2000 head, on the Laramie Plains, only two sheep died during the last winter. Of Moore & Brother's flock, consisting of over 10,000 head, only eight had died up to February 1st. All were fat, and mutton being killed every day, although the sheep had not had a mouthful to eat except the natural grasses.

HORSE-RAISING IN THE WEST.

HORSE-RAISING IN THE WEST.

CHAPTER XI.

HORSE-RAISING IN THE WEST.

Who the Horse-Raisers are—How they Manage their Herds—
Profits of Horse-Raising under Favorable Conditions—Horse
Notes.

HORSE-GROWING on the Plains has hardly yet been
established as a business; nevertheless, something has
been done, and the results show that it can be made
immensely profitable. Of the herds I have visited I
may mention those of Creighton & Alsop, Mr. T. A.
Kent, in Wyoming Territory, and Nelson A. Storey, in
Montana. Creighton & Alsop began with 300 brood-
mares. They raised a lot of yearlings, two-year-olds,
and three-year-olds, and told me they had never been
fed or sheltered. The colts were large, fat, and as fine
as could be raised anywhere. The mares were closely
herded, but never given grain or stabled in winter.
Mr. Storey began a few years ago with about 200
head of California mares, and his herd has rapidly
increased to 1300 head. His ranch is on the Upper
Yellowstone, and he neither stables nor feeds his stock.
He is a careless breeder, and takes little pains to im-

prove his stock.   The herd is looked after by one man,
and the stallions are allowed to run constantly with the
mares.   Notwithstanding the little care it has had, this
herd has improved rapidly, and its increase in numbers
has been prodigious.   Every year Mr. Storey sells off
a large number of young horses at from $50 to $75
per head, and will allow buyers to pick at $100, yet
his herd increases and is now worth a large fortune.

Mr. Kent, of Cheyenne, Wyoming Territory, has
twenty stallions, which cost him an aggregate of
$691.60 each, and some of them are very fair for
speed, but were selected especially for their breeding
qualities.   Kent is breeding by them, from California
mares, what he calls American bronchos.   They are
small, tough animals, very cheap, and good for riding,
but too light for general use or marketing for draught
purposes.   Mr. Kent's stallions weigh 1225 to 1640
pounds, and he expects the cross by them with the
California mares will reach the average size of American horses.   Size, docility, and strength are the qualities sought by Mr. Kent.   He proposes to change the
stallions every second year for a better class, and by
mixing the blood with trotters, runners, and draught
stock, to obtain from his bronchos a stock of animals
suitable for the general market.   His mares cost him
$28.50 each, and he considers his yearling colts worth
$25 each, and his two-year-olds $50 each.   He reckons
the increase at 75 to 80 per cent. per year from full-
grown mares, and, after the fourth year, 25 per cent.
of the herd.   At the commencement of the season each
stallion is coralled with about forty mares every night

for a week or more. The horse soon establishes his authority over his harem, and may be trusted to take care of it himself. He keeps his troop well together, and does not allow it to be approached or to approach and mix with another brood. He often finds himself spoiling for a fight with some other patriarch of the range, and on such occasions stops his wives at a safe distance, and goes out alone to meet the enemy. If defeated he retires in good order, driving his wives before him; but, if victorious, he looks out sharply, and, if possible, captures and drives into his harem a stray mare or two belonging to his rival. As a rule, a stud will not allow any geldings in his troop. In the fall the stallions are taken away, after which the mares have to be regularly herded.

I am indebted to Mr. Edwin Curly for the following return of Mr. Kent's ranch:

First Year.

Ranch and stables	$3,000
800 mares @ $28.50 each	22,800
20 stallions @ $691.50 each	13,830
Herding	2,500
Keeping 20 stallions	1,870
Interest @ 10 per cent. on an average investment of	
$40,000	4,000
Total	$48,000

Second Year.

Capital	$46,000
Herding	3,130
Keeping stallions	1,870
Interest of 10 per cent.	5,000
Total	$56,000

The increase, 600 or more yearling colts, is now estimated to be worth $15,000.

Third Year.

Capital account	$56,000
Herding	4,000
Keeping stallions	2,000
Interest	6,000
Total	$68,000

The increase is now estimated,—

600 two-year-old colts	$30,000
600 yearlings	15,000
Total	$45,000

Or a return in three years of the whole of the original investment, exclusive of interest. The fourth year the young stock may be estimated as worth $90,000, and from this time on one can both sell young geldings to advantage and rapidly improve the quality of his stock by breeding the young mares to a better class of stallions. I cannot give the exact figures for loss and depreciation of old stock, and the increased cost of a better class of stallions, but whatever these may be there is evidently a profit of from 25 to 33 per cent. per annum to be made by horse-breeding on the Plains. Breeding for the general market does not require any great amount of special knowledge or skill, and there is one advantage in this business in the fact that, if it is tolerably understood, a very large amount of capital may be invested and kept well in hand. One cannot personally handle with advantage one-half so much capital in cattle or a fifth as much in sheep as horses.

Some think it desirable to begin with a high class of mares, worth $100 per head, and if the horse-grower has the capital and is in a hurry to realize, undoubtedly that would be best. However, it would require $150,-000 or $200,000 to start a first-class horse-ranch of that kind, and few men have so much capital to put into any business.

As in the case of a cross between Durham bulls and Texas cows, the stallion leaves so strong an impress on his colts that the herd rapidly improves, and it can be worked up to any required standard. If I were going into horse-breeding I would at first take a low grade of mares. Many stockmen handle herds of 10,000 head of cattle, and there would be no more trouble in managing that number of horses, representing a capital of $1,500,000. One thousand mares and 200 studs would soon raise such a herd. I doubt if it would pay to engage in horse-breeding on the Plains in a very small way, unless in connection with some business, as in Kansas or Nebraska, where the mares are utilized, and made to pay for the labor, care, expense, and trouble of keeping them. Cattle-growers can use a good many mares to advantage in herding, and make them add to the profits of the herd by breeding them every year to high-graded studs. I do not know of any one who has as yet tried mule-breeding on the Plains, but undoubtedly it could be made profitable, and the government demand for army mules would furnish a steady and reliable market. Mules are the hardiest and most easily herded of all domestic animals. Of all the countries out West I have seen, the

Yellowstone Valley, I think, would be the best for horse-breeding. The climate is just right, and no shelter or feed would be required the year round. Mr. Storey's herd has done so well I am sure it is in the right place, and there is room in the Yellowstone bottoms for 200,000 head of horses to graze.

The Crow Indians, who inhabit the valley, raise the finest Indian horses I have ever seen on the Plains.

Having now written of cattle-, sheep-, and horse-growing, I will close this chapter with a few general remarks. Almost any one can make money at stock-growing, but it is one of the most laborious businesses out West, and no lazy man should ever think of trying it. A great many stock-growers fail, not because there is not money in it, but because they do not attend to their business; one drinks, another gambles, and a third allows his herd to wander off and get lost. A man to make money in stock, like other businesses, must be sober and industrious, and when the storms come he must be brave, and keep his cattle together and herd them even at the risk of his life.

In time of danger the herder must never let go his grip, or if he does the herd is ruined and the labor of years lost.

It is a life of exposure and hardship, and those who follow it industriously deserve to realize large profit from their investments and labor.

DAIRYING OUT WEST.

DAIRYING OUT WEST.

CHAPTER XII.

THE GIFT OF THE COWS.

The Growth of the Dairying *Business*—Butter and Cheese produced in the United States—Letter from a Dairyman—What can be made in the *Business*.

IN 1840 there were 4,837,043 milch-cows in the United States; in 1850 there were 6,385,094; in 1860, 8,728,863; in 1870, 11,000,000; and now about 12,000,000. In 1850 the production of butter was 313,345,306 pounds; in 1860, 469,681,372 pounds; in 1870, 560,000,000 pounds; and now about 800,-000,000 pounds. In 1860 the production of cheese was 103,663,927 pounds; in 1870, 275,000,000 pounds; and now about 400,000,000 pounds. In 1860 the United States exported 15,515,709 pounds of cheese; in 1870 they exported 70,000,000 pounds. In 1860 prime cheese sold for 11 cents per pound in New York and Boston; in 1870 it sold for 25 cents per pound. In 1860, butter averaged in Boston 21 cents per pound; in 1870, 50 cents per pound. In 1851 the first cheese-factory was started in the United States; in 1870 New

151

York alone had 1200 factories, manufacturing 100,-
000,000 pounds per annum.

Dairying, from the earliest period in American history, has been one of the most certain and remunerative
ways of making money.   Hardly a farmer's wife in the
country but has resorted to her milk, butter, and eggs
for pin-money.   How many nice things in a good
countrywoman's house have been bought with " the
marketing ?"   Thread, needles, children's shoes and
stockings, aprons, pipes, and tobacco ; these are the
natural results of a good cow, as much as butter is of
cream.   God bless old Daisy ! we owe her much, and
hardly a country boy or maiden but has worn her clothing as well as eaten her sweet butter.   On a rented
farm, with a few good cows and skilful labor, there is
no surer way to comfort, and even to small fortune, for
the little family of the new beginner.   Few people
know or can compute what colossal proportions dairying
has attained in this country in the last twenty years.
Enormous as the figures above given are, it would be
difficult to find more than half a dozen counties in the
whole United States where the supply of pure milk and
good butter is equal to the wants of the people.

Franklin County, Vermont ; Orange and Herkimer,
New York ; Chester and Lancaster, Pennsylvania ; and
Kane County, Illinois, are about the only places well
stocked with good butter, cheese, and milk.   Hardly
any other place of 3000 people can be found where the
supply equals the demand.   Even in the centre of millions of acres of rich clover pastures, surrounded by
10,000,000 agricultural people, Chicago, in one year,

bought 4,500,000 pounds of New York cheese. St. Louis is also a heavy importer from the East, and the supply of pure milk in that city is not only insufficient but the quality is very inferior. A few years ago milk sold in Mobile, Alabama, at 86 cents per gallon. Herkimer County sent out 17,000,000 pounds of cheese in one year, and 300,000 pounds of butter, worth together $4,500,000. St. Albans, Vermont, shipped 1,000,000 pounds of cheese and 2,750,000 pounds of butter, worth in market $1,200,000. Wellington, Ohio, shipped 4,000,000 pounds of cheese in one year to New York, worth $1,000,000. The country around Elgin, Illinois, produced in a single year 1,300,000 pounds of cheese, 1,600,000 quarts of milk, for the Chicago market, and 200,000 pounds of butter, the joint value of these products being $450,000. One hundred cheese-factories in New York, to which 500,000 cows were attached, produced as follows:

Value of milk from each cow	$65.50
" calf " "	10.00
Total per annum	$75.50
Deduct for manufacturing into cheese per each cow .	9.00
Average net per cow per annum	$66.50

It must be remembered, however, that in the States the cost of keeping a cow over winter is $20, which must be deducted from her annual yield. In the West this cost is wiped out, and hence 33 per cent. can be added to the profits of dairying out West over that of the Eastern States. But this is not all, for the prices are better, and 10 per cent. on that account can be added with safety.

In dairying a great deal depends on the climate, and it should be neither too hot nor too cold for the greatest success at the business. Another great desideratum is the water. Pure living streams, flowing springs, are almost indispensable to good butter making. In the West the mild air and thousands of pure gushing streams furnish multitudes of natural butter- and cheese-ranches. The melting snows not only keep the waters cool, but the snow, air, and cool nights make the milk-houses a paradise for dairy-maids. Ice can be bought as cheap if not cheaper than in the East, and every spring-house has its water-power to do the churning while the milk-maid sings her dairy-songs. Our gravelly soil, under the influence of our continued dry climate, gives the best cellars imaginable, the sides, without cost of stone walls, drying and hardening like cement.

Dr. Latham, speaking of the trans-Missouri country as a dairy-land, said: "Every stream in the trans-Missouri country is adapted to butter and cheese making. There is an unlimited market along the lines of our great railways, in our new settlements, in the great mining districts, which are scattered in the Rocky Mountains for one thousand miles north and south and nine hundred miles east and west, and at all our military posts. Besides our home demand we have a demand on the Pacific Coast. New York and Ohio annually furnish large quantities of both butter and cheese to the Pacfic Slope. The dairy product of this country would add the transportation from those States to its value here.

Mr. E. H. Derby, of Boston, one of the statisticians of the Treasury Department, 'estimates that next year China, Japan, and the Sandwich trade will buy of us, if we have it, 50,000 tons of butter and cheese;' 50,000 tons amount to 100,000,000 pounds, or if all in cheese, to the cheese product of New York State, with their 1200 factories and 500,000 milch-cows attached to them. From the sweet, nutritious character of our grasses, and from the cool, equable character of our climate, there is no reason to doubt that first-class milch-cows will produce as much butter and cheese as is produced by the same cows in the best pastures of New York, Vermont, and Ohio. The two Platte rivers drain a country which furnishes more acres of pasture than all New York State."

Mr. Curly estimates that 1200 cheese-factories in the great Platte basin, with 500,000 milch-cows, yielding $66.50 each, as they do in New York, would return to their owners, clear of all cost of manufacture, $33,-295,000. The city that could be the entrepot of such trade and traffic need not sit in sackcloth and ashes sighing for the days when the Union Pacific Railroad disbursed $2,500,000 annually.

Hutton & Alsop had 4000 cows that were kept alone to raise calves; hundreds of people saw them grazing in one herd; 4000 cows would have yielded them at New York averages, clear of all labor, $266,360. J. W. Iliff grazed on Crow Creek 3500 milch-cows, which would have yielded clear $233,065.

Dr. Latham says: "The milk of 600 cows can be manufactured in a single factory. In the States they would net for the summer $39,954; cost of wintering, at $20 per head, $12,000, leaving as actual net profits $27,000. In the great Western winter grazing-region the cost of wintering would not exceed $1 per head, or $600, leaving as the actual net profits $39,354, a difference in favor of the Plains of $11,400 on 600 cows."

Mr. Curly gives us the following interesting return of a combined dairy and stock ranch:

First Year.

Bought 50 dairy cows, @ $50	$2500
2 thoroughbred bulls	500
Expended in permanent improvements	1500
Capital :—Labor account	$4500
Expenses :—Labor, about	1500
Returns :—Butter and milk, about	1500
47 calves, valued at	500
Profit, at 11 per cent.	$2500

Second Year.

Original capital brought down	$4500
Bought 30 cows, at $50	1500
Bought 320 acres of land	800
Improvements	1000
	$7800
Expenses :—Labor	$1000
Returns :—Butter and milk	2500
Increased value, 40 yearlings become two-year-olds	500
62 calves	500
	$3500
Deduct labor	$1000
Profit, 33⅓ per cent.	$2500

In the fall of that year, after the addition of 35 brood

mares, at $44 each, 34 mixed cattle, and furniture and fixtures, to the total of $2560, the whole was valued at $15,000 for the purpose of a partnership, giving in this manner an additional profit of $4640, or 58 per cent.

Third Year.

Dairy ranch as above	$15,000 00
Bought a herd of mixed cattle at about average prices, comprising 242 yearlings, 336 two-year-olds, 294 three-year-olds, 537 beeves, 375 cows, and 16 horses ; total . . .	27,381.94
Bought two ranches	950.00
Improvements made in the year	2,410.31
Total	$45,742.25
Labor and expenses	7,200.00
Less portion of labor expended in permanent improvements	1,900.00
Total	$5,300.00
Returns :—Beef and beef cattle	$10,834.00
Butter	2,424.82
Milk	217.43
Sundries	423.39
Total	$13,899.63
Deduct expenses	5,300.00
Profit	$8,599.63

The stock remaining on hand was valued at lowest prices for an estimate of profits, those that had been wintered in the Territory being put at the prices then paid for fresh Texans. At these rates the stock on hand came to $47,054.86, from which deduct $45,742.25, and $1312.61 is left to profit account . . 1,312.61

Total profit, 21 per cent. . . .	$9,912.24

In this case the profit was undoubtedly put too low by Mr. Curly, but it was impossible to estimate it very exactly, as the herd had not been long enough in hand for that purpose.

To substantiate what I have asserted as to the adaptability of our Western grasses and climate to that branch of industry, I will close this article by some extracts from letters written by practical dairymen in the West.

Mr. Franklin Ketcham, of Cheyenne, Wyoming Territory, writes : " I have been engaged in dairying near Cheyenne, in Crow Creek Valley, for years. I started by milking five cows, and carrying the milk on foot in a pail to my customers. I added more cows to my number from time to time as the profits allowed. The second season I was milking 52 cows, all bought from the business started by the first five cows. I have found that a good dairy-cow will make as much butter or cheese from our wild grasses as in any country on tame grasses. Our cool climate is finely adapted to making both butter and cheese. I am now milking 32 cows, which are not fed either hay or grain, but graze in the valley of Crow Creek on the old dry grass. They give from thirty-six to forty gallons of milk per day. I shall add 125 cows to my present number the coming season."

Mr. W. D. Pennock writes : " I have been engaged in dairying near Cheyenne, Wyoming Territory, on a branch of Crow Creek. The first season I milked 15 cows, the next summer 32, the next year 35, and the following year 45. We sold our milk for the first six months at 30 cents per gallon. My cows averaged during that time $108 worth of milk per cow. For the next six months we sold our milk at 40 cents per gallon, and the average was as much per head as $216 per year. In winter I stable, and feed hay at night and graze during the day. I have made butter and cheese on the Western Reserve of Ohio, and I know a cow will give as much milk or make as much butter or cheese on wild grasses as she would on the richest clover and blue-grass pastures of the East."

Mr. M. Sloan writes: "I have been a dairyman in Pennsylvania, Illinois, and Montana. I commenced the same business near Cheyenne, Wyoming, many years ago. The first year I milked 20 cows, the next summer 38, the following summer 50. I have an extra lot of milch-cows for the West, and they would be called, even in the old States, first-class. For the months of June, July, and August they averaged eighteen quarts of milk daily. For the other nine months they yielded over two gallons. In the best part of the season they would make one pound and a half of butter per head daily, and the whole year they would average one pound per day. From the same cow, after acclimation, I can make more butter and cheese in the West than can be made in the most noted dairy-region in the East. Cows that are milked winters are fed on good bright hay; those that are not, graze for themselves, and are in fine order in the spring, when the milking season commences."

Mr. Edward Farrall writes: "I have been dairying at Laramie, on a branch of the Laramie River, for many years. At first I started with 20 cows. I had increased that number in a year to 40, and in two years to 60 head. From my experience I am sure that cows grazed on our Western grasses do well, and will give as much milk the year round as they will give anywhere. The milk is as rich as from any feed, and will make as much butter and cheese. Cows keep up the quantity of their milk the whole year here as well as anywhere."

I deem this evidence sufficient. All these gentlemen are well known as men of reliability in the West, and their word may be taken with implicit confidence. They all commenced poor, but now have hundreds of cattle, ranches, horses, mules, oxen, sheep, and are independent in every way. Their experience is that of hundreds of others in the West in the same business, and I could multiply scores of such letters if space permitted. Here, then, in the West is one of the widest fields of industry to the emigrant of small means. There are millions of acres of grazing the year round, where all the cows in America might be driven, and there would still be room for more. There are still thousands of unoccupied mountain streams, affording cool water for tens of thousands of dairies. The land, both grazing and timbered, can be had at government price, and the railways are reaching everywhere to carry off the dairy products, either East or West, to market. The difference between the East and the West is that there all is at a stand-still, while here something new occurs every day.

STOCK-GROWING OUT WEST.

STOCK-GROWING OUT WEST.

CHAPTER XIII.

MONTANA.

A Great State—The Chances for the Emigrant—Farmers of
Montana and what they Own—A Stock-Grower's Letter and
Experience.

JUST west of Dakota and north of Wyoming is a
very rich Territory called Montana. The climate is
delightful during the summer months, it not being too
warm, and at night a person finds it necessary to sleep
under one or more blankets. Much of the time the
atmosphere is hazy,—not unlike an Indian summer in
the Eastern States. During the winter the weather is
extremely cold, and people easily get frost-bitten by
exposure. It is never very windy, but quiet, still, cold
weather, which sometimes is exceedingly pleasant.

Montana is well named, for it is a succession of high
mountains and broad valleys. The grazing cannot be
excelled in any country in the world, and much of the
stock runs out all the winter, though there is by no
means any lack of snow. In the springtime the stock
is fat, and it is fair to say that no better beef can be
found. Horses and cattle and sheep thrive and look

fine and sleek. There is plenty of timber on the mountain-sides and in the cañons, and a thick under-growth of bushes in which there is an abundance of berries. In such a country game must abound, and here are found the moose, elk, buffalo, deer, antelope, cinnamon and black bears, badgers, beavers, martins, mink, and a variety of other wild animals.

The Crow Indians, one of the largest tribes of Indians left in the United States, live on the Yellowstone River in Montana. They still number over three thousand souls, and can muster and put in the saddle six hun-dred warriors. They are very friendly with the whites, and make it their boast that they never yet killed a white man except in self-defence. From their reser-vation they annually make their way to the buffalo hunting-grounds on the Muscleshell River, and return laden with dried meat and robes.

Montana has as yet no railroad, but many fine wagon-roads. The one leading from Corrinne, on the Central Pacific Railroad, to Helena is a fine thoroughfare, and over four hundred miles long. The road from Virginia City to Helena is also an excellent one. A road was made in the summer of 1869 from Bozeman across the country to the mouth of Muscleshell and thence back to Helena. It was thought that freight would be brought up to the mouth of the river by boats on the Missouri River and freighted across the country to such points as it might be destined for, but this has been superseded by the railroad, and now, unless the cost of carriage is too dear, the freighting will be nearly all done by the Union Pacific to Ogden, and thence by the

Utah Northern and wagons in Montana. It may cost somewhat more this way, but is more expeditions and on the whole more satisfactory to merchants and dealers. The survey of the Northern Pacific Railroad runs through Montana, and the Utah Northern is now built from Ogden to Red Rock, and will within a year reach Helena, the capital of the Territory. Over two hundred miles of this road is already in working order in Utah and Idaho, and next year it will cross Montana, possibly to the Missouri River. The enterprise is under the direction of Jay Gould, of New York, and is certain to be carried out to completion.

Montana has within her borders several rivers, the largest of which are the Missouri, Clarke's Fork of the Columbia, and the Yellowstone. The former is navigable as far as Fort Benton, but only for a few months in the year, and ordinarily boats can make but two trips from St. Louis to Fort Benton and back again during the season. The boats, however, run quite frequently between Benton and Bismarck, and the shipping interests of Montana are gradually developing. Clarke's Fork is on the west side of the Rocky Mountains, and is formed by the junction of the Bitter Root and Flat Head Rivers, the Bitter Root being itself formed by the junction of the Big Blackfoot, Missoula, and the Hellgate Rivers. The whole interior of Montana is remarkably well watered, and there are gold placers on many of the creeks, the names of which it would be useless to give, as it would only lead to confusion in obtaining a knowledge of the country. The Missouri is formed by the junction of the " Three Forks," called respectively the

Jefferson, the Madison, and the Gallatin Rivers, so named by Lewis and Clarke.

These are all noble streams, filled with trout, lined with fine growths of timber, and bordered by beautiful and fertile valleys. In the Madison are found the grayling or "half trout," a peculiar kind of fish which has specks and scales, being half trout and half whitefish. The timber and underbrush along the streams are a favorite resort for Indians, who are now friendly. It is somewhat singular that no hard wood, such as hickory and maple, are found west of the Rocky Mountains.

The many ranges of mountains in the Territory gave it its name, and long before the whites came it was known to the Snake or Schoshonee Indians as " Toyabe-schock-up," or " The Country of the Mountains." The only considerable body of water is Flat-Head Lake, in the northwestern corner of the Territory, and it is the source of the river of that name.

The best valleys in Montana are the Gallatin, Missoula, and Yellowstone. The Gallatin as an agricultural valley is second only to the Lancaster in Pennsylvania. In Missoula fifty bushels of wheat are readily raised per acre. The Yellowstone is already famous for its fine vegetable productions. Plums, peaches, apples, apricots, and all kinds of vines and berries thrive in Southern Montana. Wild fruits, such as currants, gooseberries, raspberries, buffalo berries, sarvice berries, and plums, are found in many parts of the Territory and of excellent quality. The Indians use these for food, drying large quantities and mixing them with the marrow of buffalo bones for winter use; the dried berries are sometimes pounded up with buffalo meat and fat, making a sort of " pemmican," which is packed in skins and called " towro."

I have been thus particular in describing the natural and agricultural resources of Montana, because it is only known to the outside world as a mining region. The commonly received idea of it is that it is a wild, rugged, and unproductive territory, valuable only for its gold and silver. Could it once be made known that for agricultural purposes it will some day be as valuable as Nebraska, Iowa, or Minnesota, new life would be given to this rock-bound land, and its valleys would soon fill up with thrifty farmers.

It is, however, as a stock-growing region Montana surpasses all other sections of our great West. Its grasses cure naturally on the ground, and even in winter cattle and sheep, which run out all the year round, are found fat and fit for the butcher's block.

In 1877 the whole number and value of live stock in Montana was set down by the assessors as follows:

	Number.	Value.
Cattle	160,647	$1,812,920
Horses	26,496	851,674
Mules	1,688	105,648
Sheep	51,558	148,894
Hogs	4,642	20,598
Total	245,031	$2,939,734

Since then the stock in Montana has more than doubled, Gallatin County alone returning, in 1879, 30,333 head of cattle and 8033 head of horses. Among the owners of herds in Gallatin are the following:

Owner.	Number.
S. H. Many	103
John McDonald	300
W. F. McCormack	112
J. H. Nixon	75
Joseph Neihart	50
Sanford Ruffner	175
E. Ryan	364
H. B. Ray	100
H. C. Reding	55
Milo Seketer	150
Nelson Story	1300
James Smart	225
Street Brothers	65
John Simpson	50
Leroy Southland	135
Stanton & Pease	425
A. J. Smith	72
W. F. Sloan	300
Ben Gallagher	100
Ben Strickland	143
H. H. Sappington	164
Philip Thorpe	600
J. H. Tinsel	86
C. W. Haskins	120
T. C. Hamilton	55
William Hunkinson	63
R. D. Hamilton	60
Alf. Johnson	160
William M. James	200
Joseph Jackson	58
Lee & Cone	500
L. A. Lune	231
J. M. Lindley	122
Sampson Landes	128
Peter Lebeau	65
G. S. Lewis	72
Freeman Mize	188
J. D. McCammon	140

Owner.	Number.
Daniel Maxey	140
A. B. Moore	70
W. A. Minor	67
D. A. Moore & Brother	138
James M. Moore	86
George Allan	312
Charles Anceney	252
J. W. Alexander	175
W. M. Anderson	175
Brooks Brothers	100
L. M. Black	70
Frank Baïne	69
T. C. Burns	57
S. A. Bostwick	42
William Black	62
James Burrell	40
H. Bemer	85
J. C. Batie	120
John Baptiste	45
Martin & Myers	1300
R. B. Curtis	60
W. W. Curtis	57
James Cummings	50
Andy Cowan	75
J. M. Conrow	103
H. F. Galen	95
E. M. Dumphy	445
G. L. Duke	52
E. Daily	128
F. Edmunds	70
M. J. Eukes	54
C. Etherington	52
S. M. Fitzgerald	99
Wm. Fly	200
David Fratt	240
J. A. Farrall	70
John W. Grannis	157
J. H. Gallup	130

Owner.	Number.
H. N. Gage	98
G. L. Condon	152
L. *B.* Galter	298
James Green	125
M. V. Harris	100
Francis Harper	115
Henry Heebe	70
Hutchinson *Brothers*	60
John Harvey	60
J. O. Hopping	61
Tritt & Kountz	90
James Uhler	66
Wm. M. Wright	220
H. J. Wright	347
Frank Wells	200
J. R. Wilson	125
A. D. Weaver	64
G. W. Wakefield	50
John White	90
James White	130

It will be observed that most of these owners are new beginners, and have as yet but small herds. The immense profits to be derived from stock-growing in Montana are just beginning to be understood, and every ranchman who can get together a few head of cattle, sheep, or horses is going at it. Among the owners of horse-ranches in Gallatin County I find the names of the following gentlemen:

Owner.	Number.
Nelson Story	1200
Henry Heebe	140
George Gardes	400
C. Ethrington	42
D. M. Murphy	45
G. H. Campbell	45

Owner.	Number.
W. M. Cowan	132
V. A. Cockrell	70
Martin & Myers	91

These are also new beginners, except Mr. Story. Horses do so well in Montana that the growing of them is rapidly becoming one of the settled businesses of the Territory.

There is a famous range for cattle on Sun River, in the northern part of Montana, and over 100,000 head are grazed there. Among the owners of herds are the following:

Owner.	Number.
Jake Smith & Brother	200
Samuel Ford	400
Frank Goss	200
Clarke & Elen	10,000
Con Korrs	6,000
Flory & Cox	6,000
Wm. Mulchaey	700
Mrs. N. Ford	300
Robert Ford	3,000
O. H. Churchill	6,000
Matt Furnell	400
Burnett Murray	400
Robert Vaughan	300
Samuel Bird	600
Mane & Dennis	500
James Gibson	600
T. J. Stocking	3,000
M. W. Wyatt	500
Isaac Kingsberry	600
Rufus J. Harding	500
Lepley & Austin	2,000
Kipp & Thomas	600
Sargent & Steele	350

Of the herds on the south side of the Missouri there are 20,000; on Flat Creek and on Dearborne, 10,000; and on the smaller streams fully 2000 head.

The governor of the Territory, Hon. B. F. Potts, is one of the most successful sheep-growers in Montana, and owns large herds. General A. J. Smith is also a large owner of this kind of stock.

I have visited many of the stock-ranches and conversed with their owners, and all seem highly pleased with their experience as stock-growers. They have large expectations of future profits, and some of the heaviest owners declared they would not exchange their herds for the best gold-mine in the Territory. The profit on herds is estimated at from 26 to 48 per cent. on the capital invested, and, large as this may seem, I do not think it too high for realization.

H. F. Galen, a practical stock-grower, writing recently to the author, states:

"I bought my sheep, in the fall of 1876, of Mr. Calhoun, who drove them in from Nevada. There were 3500 head in the flock. I afterwards sold 1000 head to Mr. Hussey, who is a sheep-grower on Smith River. In consequence of my inexperience, I leased the remaining 2500 to the Smith Brothers, on Crow Creek, who are worthy gentlemen. They, too, had little experience in sheep, and the herd took the scab very bad the first year and did not do well. We lost half of the lambs by their being dropped in winter. Out of over 1200 lambs we only saved 785. Of wool we had only 7000 pounds. Last year we did not turn in our bucks with the ewes until the 6th of December, and then we dipped the sheep in a solution of strong lye and tobacco, and they did well. I believe we will have a better crop of both lambs and wool this year than ever before, and we expect to clip at least four pounds of fleece per head. I have a grain-ranch at Willow Creek, Montana, where I keep my cattle principally. I have let the ranch on shares, but my cattle are in my own possession. I have 200 head. I cannot give you much information about cattle, as I pay most attention to horses. I have 75 brood-mares and 3 stallions, which I keep in the stables for breeding purposes. I keep the mares herded from the first of May until the middle of August, when they are turned out and bred for the balance of the year. The stable-stallions are well kept and groomed. The mares are led out to them, each mare booked, and her colt recorded. I endeavor to improve the breed by putting horses to mares that are no kin to them. I castrate and halter and break my colts every spring, when they are one year old. At three years of age they are put into harness or under the saddle. I have sold but few horses or cattle since I commenced the stock-raising business. If I were to sell out, I think after deducting losses I could realize 30 per cent. per annum on my investment out of my sheep, and 25 per cent. on my horses. My sheep are mixed between Spanish merino and cotswold. I think they are a very good lot, but suppose the Spanish merino to be the best. I expect they will clip over four pounds of wool to each sheep this year. I believe the sheep I sold Mr. Hussey will do better than that. I feed no hay in winter, except to my stallions and some of my fine brood-mares. I think the Smith Brothers feed a very little hay to such of their sheep as need extra care. They have sheds to protect them from the storms.

"I believe Montana is as good as any country in the world for stock of any kind. It is peculiarly adapted to sheep on account of the dryness of the climate. All that is needed is a good shepherd and experience to cure sheep of scab, and the herd will thrive. The scab is the only disease I know of prevalent among the sheep of Montana. I have made no changes in either bucks or ewes in my herds since I commenced raising. Mr. Burt has bought all the sheep he could get afflicted with scab, and cures them in a short time. It appears to be a disease easily cured when one comes to understand it.

"H. F. GALEN,
"*Stock Grower.*"

Charles Cook, of Cook Brothers, who are very experienced herdsmen, writes to me:

"Our ranch is located on Smith River, in Smith River Valley, eighteen miles from Camp Baker, Montana. We have been in business since July, 1873. We have 1300 head, 900 of them ewes. They were for the most part common, ungraded ewes and rams, with coarse wool. I drove them from Oregon to Montana. We have made no additional purchases to the herd since starting it, and have sold about $4000 worth of mutton and wool, as follows:

"Old ewes	$1000
Graded rams	1700
Wool	1700

WAITING FOR THE FOG TO CLEAR.

"We have now on hand 6000 head of graded sheep. In February, 1877, we purchased in company with another grower 2500 head, and last March another lot of 1800 for new herds. Both these bands are doing well. The rate of profit is hard to estimate, as that depends upon economy, judicious management, and the grade of sheep raised. A herd of 3000 head of well-graded ewes ought to raise 80 per cent. lambs. We have raised 100 per cent. this year. Each sheep will clip from $1.25 to $1.50 worth of wool per annum. Fifty per cent. will herd and keep them, and 5 per cent. will cover all losses. Our losses during the past year have been less than 2 per cent. We have used nothing but pure-blood cotswold rams in our flocks; I believe they are the best, and adapted to our climate. They seem to stand our cold weather well, and in deep snows they have length of limbs and strength of body to wade through it and paw for food. They are very prolific, and make excellent nurses. Their lambs are dropped large, strong, and well wooled. The merinos are directly the opposite in all these points. They are not prolific, nor are they careful nurses; their lambs are born small, weak, and naked. Our lambing seasons are subject to severe storms and cold nights. These are my observations in handling both coarse- and fine-wooled sheep. Our graded sheep clip an average of six pounds per head. The original herd clipped only four pounds. We have never fed any hay, and make no provision for feeding further than to keep the winter range fresh. For shelter we put up a wall of logs and cover them with poles and hay, which makes a sufficient protection against all storms of winter. *We have never lost any sheep from severe weather in Montana.*

"The only disease which sheep are subject to in this country is scab, and I do not consider that indigenous to the climate. When once cured they remain so, unless they come in contact with diseased animals. The remedies I use for curing scab are lime, sulphur, carbolic and hemlock dip with tobacco, as it is perfectly harmless to the sheep and the fleece, and a sure cure for the disease if rightly applied.

"I consider Montana one of the best wool-growing sections of the United States. Our ranges are extensive, our grasses nutritious and abundant, while pure water is found on every hillside and in every valley. California has its floods, droughts, and famines; Oregon its leeches and scab; Nevada and Utah their alkali plains and brackish waters, which affect the wool of sheep as well as their health. The soft alluvial deposits of many parts of the West produce foot-rot. We in Montana alone are free from all these, and I see no reason why this should not become the greatest stock- and wool-growing region in the world.

"Chas. W. Cook."

It is, however, as a blooded-stock region Montana takes the lead. Notwithstanding its remoteness, it already has a larger number and better quality of blooded horses and cattle than any State or Territory in the Northwest. Of its blooded ranches I shall have to speak in another chapter.

A visit to the blooded-stock farms of Montana will

convince any one that this distant Territory of the great West is destined to become in the near future second only to Kentucky for fine stock. It is astonishing, the progress it has made during the last five years in breeding blooded animals of all kinds. I have visited many of the stud- and cattle-farms, and find them superior to all others in the West. The careful breeding of Montana owners must in the end, if persevered in, give the Territory a stock of horses and cattle that cannot be surpassed by any in this country.

Poindexter & Orr have a fine herd of thoroughbred cattle near Watson, Montana, which they imported from Canada. In 1872 they commenced with five bulls and eight heifers, short-horn Durhams. They are set down in the stock books as follows:

BULLS.

1. *Lobo Lad.* Raised by John Zavitz. Recorded vol. ii. Canadian Herd Book, p. 146, and purchased by us May, 1872. No. 1661.

2. *Bismark.* Bred by Robert White, London Township, Middlesex County, Canada. Recorded vol. ii. Canadian Herd Book, page 294. No. 2476.

3. *General Napier.* Bred by J. B. Lane, Dorchester County, Middlesex, Canada. Recorded vol. ii. Canadian Herd Book, page 109. No. on herd book, 1467.

4. *London Duke.* Recorded vol. iii. Canadian Herd Book; tried by Thomas Elliott, Arva Township, County Middlesex, Canada.

5. *King William.* Sold to L. Born of Beaverhead County, who has certificate of registry.

m -

COWS.

1. (Imported by Poindexter & Orr from Canada, 1872.) *Cherry.* Bred by Thomas Friendship. Recorded vol. ii. Canadian Herd Book, page 385. Red roan. Calved May 9, 1867.

2. *Victoria.* Bred by Thomas Friendship, London Township, Middlesex County. Recorded vol. ii. Canadian Herd Book, page 815. Red and white. Calved Nov. 5, 1867.

3. *Daisy.* Bred by Thomas Friendship, London, Middlesex County, Canada. Recorded vol. ii. Canadian Herd Book, page 410. Red roan. Calved Jan. 16, 1871.

4. *Lobo Lass.* Bred by Joseph Walker, London Township, County Middlesex. Recorded vol. ii., page 603. Red and white. Calved Jan. 25, 1871.

5. *Fanny.* Bred by Thomas Friendship, London, Middlesex County, Canada. Recorded vol. ii. Canadian Herd Book, page 465. Roan. Calved March 20, 1871.

6. *Cherry in the Forest.* Bred by John Little, Ilderton Township, Middlesex County, Canada. Recorded Canadian Herd Book, vol. ii., page 387. Red roan. Calved Jan. 6, 1871.

7. *Alma.* Bred by William J. Hill, Dorchester Township, County Middlesex. Recorded vol. ii. Canadian Herd Book, page 332. Light roan. Calved Feb. 10, 1871. Twin.

8. *Lily.* Twin of No. 7; died 1874.

The produce from the above-named cows has been as follows:

From Cherry.

1st calf, bull Duke Beaverhead, calved Jan. 12, 1873.
2d " heifer Imogene, " Dec. 1, 1873.
3d " heifer Roan Cherry, " Nov. 30, 1874.
4th " bull Don Pedro, " Jan. 10, 1876.
5th " bull (died), " Jan. 1877.

From Victoria.

1st calf, bull Joachim Miller, calved March 10, 1873.
2d " heifer Beatrice, " " 19, 1874.
3d " bull H. W. Beecher, " Feb. 12, 1875.
4th " Louisa Lorne, " March 14, 1876.

From Daisy.

1st calf, heifer Nelly Grant, calved March 3, 1873.
2d " bull St. Patrick, " " 17, 1874.
3d " " Telton, " April 5, 1875.
4th " heifer Daisy Dean, " Feb. 23, 1876.

From Cherry in the Forest.

1st calf, heifer Phœbe Cozzens, calved April 3, 1873.
2d " " Minnie Myrtle, calved March 28, 1874.
3d " " died in calving, March, 1875.
4th " bull Gov. Hayes, calved Jan. 12, 1877.

From Fanny.

1st calf, bull Brick Pomeroy, calved March 16, 1873.
2d " " Gold Hunter, " April 5, 1874.
3d " " Mounted Lad, " March 30, 1875.
4th " heifer Peach Bloom, " April 8, 1876.
5th " bull Humpy Dumpy, " March 5, 1877.

From Lobo Lass.

1st calf, heifer Annie Laurie, calved April 14, 1873.
2d "   "   Mary Queen Scots, calved March 28, 1874.
3d " bull F. K. Moulton, calved April 15, 1875.
4th "   " Fortune,   "   March 27, 1876.

From Lily.

1st calf, heifer Orphan Lily, calved June 10, 1874.

From Nelly Grant.

1st calf, heifer Beauty, calved May 10, 1875.
2d "   "   Mountain Rose, calved March 3, 1876.
3d " bull Red Cloud,   "   May 7, 1877.

From Annie Laurie.

1st calf, bull Rob Roy, calved May 1, 1875.
2d "   "   Bobby Burns, calved March 30, 1876.
3d "   "   Bruce,   "   June 10, 1877.

From Phœbe Cozzens.

1st calf, heifer Phœbe Jane, calved March 7, 1876.

From Imogene.

1st calf, heifer Euphemia, calved March 29, 1876.

From Fanny Myrtle.

1st calf, bull Alexis, calved March 6, 1876.

From Beatrice.

1st calf, bull Prince Albert, calved March 10, 1876.
2d "   "   Prince Alfred,   "   June 1, 1877.

From Orphan Lily.

1st calf, bull Bristow, calved March 25, 1876.
2d "   heifer White Rose, calved June 26, 1877.

From Mary Queen Scots.

1st calf, heifer Darchulia, calved April 12, 1876, making an increase of 46 head from spring of 1873 to 1878. Some 8 or 10 calves are yet to come this season, which will increase the produce from the 8 cows and heifers brought to Montana in May, 1872, to about 55 head. It will be observed that in 1872 there was no increase, being mostly one- and two-year-old heifers. Mr. Orr says in a letter to the author, " I am convinced that no more profitable or productive class of stock could be brought to the Territory than short-horned thorough-breds."

Speaking for the firm, he adds: " We are of the opinion that blooded-stock breeding will eventually be one of the greatest interests in Montana. With the healthiest stock-climate in the world, the purest water, and the best feed, there is nothing to prevent Montana from taking the front rank in the production of fine stock.

" We estimate our herd of thoroughbreds to be worth at least $12,000 to $15,000. In vols. ii. and iii., C. H. B., and vol. xv., A. H. B., will be found most of our herd records.   Our experience teaches us that half and three-quarter breeds are as good 'wrestlers' in winter as 'scrub-stock.'   We have been engaged in stock-raising for more than twenty years in California, Oregon, and Montana, raising cattle, sheep, and horses, and we are convinced that Montana is far ahead of any other section with which we are acquainted for stock-raising."

Sedman & McGregory's blooded-stock farm is nearly as extensive as Poindexter & Orr's.   They have, among others, the following fine animals:

BULLS.

Kansas Clay, 8449, A. H. Book.—Bred by Charles T. Redman, Clark Co., Kentucky.   Calved May 4, 1869.   Got by Burnside, 4618, out of Linda Clay by Haverlock, 2598; Linda by Kansas, 3046; Almira by Belmont, 242; Elvira by Prince Albert 2d, 857; America by Locomotive, 92 (4242); imp. Lady Elizabeth by Emperor (1974); Elvira by Duke (1933), by Wellington (2824), by Young Remus (2522), by Midas (435), by Traveller (655), by Bolingbroke (86).

Ethelbert, No. 10,019, A. H. Book, vol. x.—Red and white.   Bred by William Warfield, Lexington, Kentucky.   Calved July 19, 1870.   Got by imp. Robert Napier (27,310), 8975; 1st dam Eleanor Townley by imp. Challenger, 324; 2d dam Miss Townley by Reneck, 903; 3d dam Miss Nanny by Prince Albert 2d, 857; 4th dam Red Beauty by John Randolph, 603; 5th dam Hannah Moore by imp. Goldfinder (2066); 6th dam imp. Young Mary by Jupiter (2170); 7th dam Mary by Saladin (1417); 8th dam Lucy by Meeks Bull (2288); 9th dam bred by Mr. Holmes, of Ottington, England.

Lord Lovell (17,574), A. H. Book.—Red roan. Bred by Walter Handy, Mount Freedom, Jessamine Co., Kentucky, the property of Stedman & McGregory, Nevada, Madison Co., Montana. Calved in September, 1870. Got by Vivian, 9272, out of Alba 2d by Ben Nevis (6451); Alba by Minstrel, 5960; Winter Rose by Valentine, 1060; Cherry by Bulwer, 300, by Oliver, 2387; Nancy Dawson by Sam Martin, 2599; Lady Kate by Tecumseh, 5409; Mrs. Motte by Adam (717), etc.

cows.

Inez 3d, A. H. B., vol. viii., page 383. Red. Calved March, 1877. Got by Rama, 7158, out of Inez 2d by Ben Nevis, 6451; Inez by Minstrel, 5960; Jane Grey by Young Oliver (2441); Nancy Dawson 3d by Bulwer, 300; Nancy Dawson 2d by Duke of York (1941); Nancy Dawson by Sam Martin (2599); Lady Kate by Tecumseh (5409); Mrs. Motte by Adam (717); bred to Vivian (9272).

Sallie Meadows, A. H. B., vol. ix., page 948. Red roan. Bought of Walter Handy. Got by the Meadows Duke, 9200; Nanny Goodloe by Duke of Argyll, 5539; Bellflower by Seaton, 4356; Susannah by Prince Hal, 3302; Cranberry by Locomotive, 645; Mary Tompkins by Comet, 356, by Accommodation (2907), imp. White Rose by Publicold, 1348; Fanny by Premier (1331), by Pilot (495), by Agamemnon (9), by Marshal Beresford (415).

Emma Kendall, A. H. B., vol. xiii., page 574.   Red
and white.   Bred by S. P. Kenny, Lexington, Kentucky, the property of Sedman & McGregory, Nevada,
Madison Co., Montana.   Calved March 3, 1870.   Got
by Campbell, 9592, out of Ella by Duke Amelek
(6616); Minnie by Orontes 3 (3226); Mattie Wright
by Allen (2492); Pocahontas by Achilles, 2471; Adelaide 2d by Comet (356); Beauty of Wharfdale by
Brutus (1752); Adelaide by Magnum Bonum (2243);
Beauty by George (1066), by Lancaster (260), by Lancaster (360), by Wellington (680), by George (275), by
Favorite (252), by Punch (531).

Lizzie, A. H. B., vol. xiii., page 728.   Red and white.
Bred by S. P. Kenny, Jessamine Co., Kentucky, the
property of Sedman & McGregory, Nevada, Madison
Co., Montana.   Calved November 12, 1869.   Got by
Gratz (14,412) out of Lucina by Royal Arch, 7230;
Graceful by John O'Groat (1707); Magnolia by Don
John (426); Moss Rose by Eclipse (1494); Miss Points,
Jr., by Northern Light (1280); Points by Aide-de-
Camp (722), by Charles (127), by Prince (521), by
Neswick (1266).

In a communication to the author, Messrs. Sedman
& McGregory say, " We have been in the business
nearly six years, and our increase from the original
number of thoroughbreds imported by us from Kentucky (which number consisted of three bulls and
four cows) has been 26 head, of which 25 are living,
and the pedigree in brief form of these 25 head is
given below.

"We bought, in the year 1871, in Missouri, 156

head of yearling heifers (common stock). In 1872 we purchased an additional number (206 head) of the same kind, sex, and age, making our total purchases of common stock equal 362 head. We have sold and killed about 200 head from the increase of the above 362 head, and our herd now numbers 1500 head ; and by the use of our thoroughbreds and grade-bulls we have improved the herd and increased the value of the stock we have raised from $2 to $5 per head, at the present low market-price. From our thoroughbreds we have raised 25 head, of which 10 are bulls and 15 cows, and the pedigree and names of these 25 head are as follows, to wit:

" From *Inez* 3d we have raised the following animals, to wit:

"*Alpha,* got by Vivian, 9272, vol. xiii., page 443, A. H. B. Prince Albert, 18,006, got by Kansas Clay, 8449. Inez Clay, A. H. B., vol. xiv., page 576, got by Kansas Clay, 8449. Inez Clay, 2d, A. H. Book, vol. xiv., page 576, got by Kansas Clay, 8449. Fanny Lovell, got by Lord Lovell, 17,574.

"*From Alpha* we have raised Alfaretta, A. H. B., vol. xiii., page 438, got by Ethelbert, 10,019.

"*From Alfaretta* we have raised Ada, got by Ethelbert, 10,019.

"*From Sallie Meadows* we have raised Pocahontas, A. H. Book, vol. xiii., page 558, got by Corporal, 7760. Captain Clay, got by Kansas Clay, 8449. Lady Sheridan, got by Ethelbert, 10,019. A bull calf, got by Ethelbert, 10,019.

"*From Pocahontas* we have raised H. P. Napier, got

by Ethelbert, 10,019.   Ex. got by Ethelbert, 10,019.
A cow calf, got by Captain Clay, 16,395.

"*From Lady Sheridan* we have raised a cow calf, got
by Ethelbert, 10,019.

"*From Lizzie* we have raised Champion, 16,451, got
by Kansas Clay, 8449.   Stella, A. H. Book, vol. xiv.,
page 872, got by Ethelbert, 10,019.   Don Juan, got by
Ethelbert, 10,019.   Two bull calves, got by Ethelbert,
10,019.

"*From Stella* we have raised a cow calf, got by Ethelbert, 10,019.

"*From Emma Kendall* we have raised Ethelbert 2d,
17,057, got by Ethelbert, 10,019.   Maud, A. H. B.,
vol. xiv., page 708, got by Ethelbert, 10,019.   Chance,
a cow calf, got by Captain Clay, 16,395; and one cow
calf, got by Lord Lovell, 17,574.

" Our experience with our thoroughbreds has been
that low, heavy, compact, and square-bodied bulls of
the 'Booth' strain of blood are the best to cross with
common stock.   All the use and purpose of the importation of thoroughbred stock to this Territory at the
present time is to improve common stock and increase
its value.

" Our ranch is situated on upper Ruby Valley, on
Ruby River, in this (Madison) county, about twenty
miles south of Virginia City, and contains about two
thousand acres under fence, with good and substantial
dwellings, stables, barns, corrals, out-houses, etc., etc.,
and the range for grazing extends from our premises a
distance of several miles in all directions.

" Ruby River runs through our ranch, and is kept

entirely free from ice during the winter by water issuing from the warm springs, which are several miles distant from our premises.

"The raising of thoroughbred stock in this Territory is as yet in its infancy; there has not been and is not now that care taken here with them as there is in older settled communities. Nearly all our thoroughbred stock are turned into pastures, and remain there during the whole year. During the severe storms of winter they have access to straw-stacks and shelter, and they keep in good order all the time.

"Our thoroughbred stock raised in this manner is fully as good as that which we imported from Kentucky.

"Our herd of thoroughbred stock is probably worth about $4000.

"In conclusion, we would say that we now have some 1500 head of common stock ; that we employ from one to two men constantly as herders ; we cut and put up one hundred tons of hay per annum, nearly all of which we feed to horses and stock on the ranch.

"Among the stock on the ranch to which we feed hay are included a number of dairy cows. Our losses of common stock from eating poisoned weeds during the spring, from exposure during the winter, and from all other causes, excepting that hereinafter mentioned, have not exceeded one per cent.

"Losses of calves that have been dropped during the very severe storms of winter are not included in the foregoing statement.

"Last season we raised 375 calves, and lost only some

8 or 10 by their being dropped in very stormy weather.

"As items of interest to you we would state that in March, A.D. 1877, we had a calf dropped from one of our common-stock cows that weighed one hundred and twelve pounds when it was only thirty-six hours old, and it was a healthy and well-formed calf. Also, that in April, 1876, we sold to butchers a barren cow, the meat of which weighed nine hundred and three pounds net.

" This was after a severe winter, and the cow had been on the range all winter. This will serve to show you the nutritious qualities of our grasses during a severe winter."

C. E. Williams, of Helena, Montana, has some fine blooded horses and mares, among others,

Caribou.

Bay horse. Bred by A. J. Alexander, Woodburn Farm, Spring Station, Kentucky. Foaled, 1870.

By Lexington.

1st dam, Alice Jones, by imp. Glencoe.
2d　"　Blue Bonnett, by imp. Hedgford.
3d　"　Grey Fanny, by Bertrand.
4th　"　by imp. Buzzard.
5th　"　Arminda, by imp. Medley.
6th　"　by imp. Bolton.
7th　"　Sallie Wright, by Yorick.
8th　"　Jenny Cameron, by imp. Childers.

9th dam by Morton's imp. Traveller.
10th " Imp. Jenny Cameron, by a son of Fox.
11th " Miss Belvoir, by Gray Grantham.
12th " by Puget Turk.
13th " Betty Percival, by Leede's Arabian.
14th " by Spanker.

No. 1. *Terlulia.*

Bay. Bred by Major B. G. Thomas, Lexington, Kentucky. Foaled, 1874.

By *Melbourn, Jr.*

1st dam, Varsouvienne, by imp. Australian.
2d " Geneva, by Lexington.
3d " Grisette, by imp. Glencoe.
4th " Fandango, by imp. Leviathan.
5th " Imp. Gallopade, by Catton.
6th " Camillina, by Camillus.
7th " by Smolensko.
8th " Miss Cannon, by Orville.
9th " by Weathercock.
10th " Cora, by Matchem.
11th " by Turk.
12th " by Cub.
13th " by Allworthy.
14th " by Starling.
15th " by Bloody Buttocks.
16th " by Greyhound.
17th " Brocklesby Betty, by Curwen's Bay Barb.
18th " Leede's Hobby mare, by Sister Barb.

No. 2. *Juggle.*

Bay.   Bred by Major B. G. Thomas, Lexington, Kentucky.   Foaled, 1874.

By Melbourn, Jr.

1st dam, Mary Hadley, by O'Meara.
2d   "   Parisina, by imp. Leviathan.
3d   "   Marie Shelby, by Stockholder.
4th "   Patty-puff, by Pocolet.
5th "   Rosa Clack, by imp. Saltram.
6th "   Jet, by Haynes' Flimnap.
7th "   Camilla, by Melzar.
8th "   Diana, by Clodius.
9th "   Sally Painter, by Evans' imp. Sterling.
10th "   Imp. Silver, by Belsize Arabian.
11th "   by Croft's Partner.
12th "   Sister to Roxana, by Bald Galloway.
13th "   Sister to Chanter, by Akaster Turk.
14th "   by Leede's Arabian.
15th "   by Spanker.

No. 3. *Artistic.*

Chestnut.   Bred by T. J. Montague, Lexington, Kentucky.   Foaled, 1874.

By Imp. Australian.

1st dam, Maud Tauris, by imp. Yorkshire.
2d   "   Rosemary, by imp. Sovereign.
3d   "   Beta, by imp. Leviathan.

₄4th dam Juliet, by Kosciusko.

  5th "   Blank, by Sir Archy.

  6th "   Imp. Psyche, by Sir Peter Teazle.

  7th "   Bab, by Bordeaux.

  8th "   Speranza, by Eclipse.

  9th "   Virago, by Snap.

10th "   by Regulus.

11th "   sister to Black and All Black, by Crab.

12th "   Miss Slammerkin, by Young True Blue.

13th "   by Lord Oxford's dun Arabian.

14th "   D'Arcy's black-legged Royal Mare.

No. 4. *Reply*

Bay. Bred by H. P. McGrath, Lexington, Kentucky. Foaled, 1872.

By Enquirer.

1st dam, Colleen Bawn, by Endorser.

  2d "   Roxana, by imp. Chesterfield.

  3d "   Levia, by imp. Tranby.

  4th "   Tolivia, by imp. Contract.

  5th "   Diamond, by Turpin's Florizel.

  6th "   by Levis's Eclipse.

  7th "   Minerva, by Melzar.

  8th "   by Union.

  9th "   Kirtly mare, by Madison's Milo.

10th "   by imp. Fearnought.

11th "   a thoroughbred mare.

There are, besides these, some fifteen other blooded-stock farms in Montana of which I might give a particular account, but to speak of all in detail would swell the size of this chapter beyond its proper proportions, and the above will serve as samples of the rest.

In regarding Montana the reader must remember that this Territory is now almost isolated from the great and stirring events which are going on in the new path of commerce which stretches across the continent. It seems to be, and really is, one of the most remote portions of our country, blocked in by the far Western States and those of the Pacific, and having for its boundary on the north the bleak and almost limitless British possessions.

It is a majestic, wild, and solitary land, embracing that region lying between the 45th and 49th parallels of north latitude and the 27th and 39th meridians west from Washington. It contains an area of 143,766 square miles,—equal to 92,016,640 acres,—extending from east to west about 750 miles, and from north to south about 275 miles. This area is nearly equal to that of California, and three times that of New York.

Of this region the surveyor-general, in his report for 1869, estimates that fully 30,672,216 acres are susceptible of cultivation.

This is about one-third of the Territory. The other two-thirds comprise the main range of the Rocky Mountains, running north and south across the Territory, and numerous subordinate spurs, whose peaks often surpass in altitude those of the main range.

Among the spurs may be mentioned the Cœur d'Alene and Bitter Root Mountains, making the dividing-line between Montana and Idaho on the west,

A QUIET INSPECTION.

between which and the main range lies the rich and productive country embraced in Deer Lodge and Missoula Counties; the Belt and Judith Mountains, separating the sparsely-settled Muscleshell County on the northeast and Choteau County on the northwest from the rich mining regions of Meagher County on the south, extending to the Missouri River, which is also the northeastern boundary of Lewis and Clark County; the Bear's Paw and Little Rocky Mountains, still to the north; the Big Horn Mountains, extending into Dakota, in the southeast, north and east of which lies the unorganized county of Big Horn or Vaughan, embracing the Yellowstone region, with Gallatin County to the northwest, and Madison and Beaverhead lying west and southwest; and the western spurs of the Wind River Mountains on the extreme eastern border.

Coal of a good quality has been found in Montana, and as rapidly as the country settles up and it becomes necessary to develop this source of wealth it will, no doubt, be found in great abundance, and perhaps of a superior quality. Near Bozeman a fine vein of bituminous coal has been developed. Just above Benton a promising vein has been opened; above Bannock, and also near Virginia City and on the Dearborn, veins of from four to five feet have been discovered.

The inhabitants of Montana are a generous, open-hearted people, full of life and activity, and noted for that boundless hospitality which is peculiar to the frontier. They change their places of abode readily, build up a town rapidly and with little or no ceremony, and abandon it as readily with no symptoms of regret.

Wherever mines are, there are they also. They believe in themselves; take an immense amount of stock in the Great West; do not object to " whiskey straight;" are always on hand to assist a friend in distress; and take kindly to theatres and saloons. It is not a good place for ladies to come who wish to keep single. There are so many bachelors a young lady finds herself surrounded at once with suitors, and some of the applicants will not be put off. In many parts of the Territory plug hats and store clothes are still the abomination of the Montanian. A buckskin rig, in the mountains, is considered the height of fashion, with a broad-brimmed soft hat reared back in front.

APPENDIX.

APPENDIX.

CATTLE-RAISING IN COLORADO.

JUDGE DAVID W. SHERWOOD, of Connecticut, recently wrote to Wilkes' "Spirit":

"EDITOR *Spirit of the Times*,—In a recent issue of the 'Spirit' I see General Brisbin, U.S.A., your valuable correspondent on 'Cattle-Growing out West,' writes as follows :

" 'I have often thought if some enterprising person would form a joint-stock company for the purpose of breeding, buying, and selling horses, cattle, and sheep, it would prove enormously profitable. I have no doubt but a company properly managed would declare an annual dividend of at least 25 per cent. Such a company, organized with a president, secretary, treasurer, and board of directors, and conducted on strictly business principles, would realize a far larger profit on the money invested than if put into any other kind of business. Nothing, I believe, would beat associated capital in the cattle trade. The ranches and ranges should be located with a view of ultimately buying the land or securing control of it for a long term of years.'

" I have for some time held the same opinion as your correspondent, but it never struck me so forcibly as

when on my ranch this spring. I saw so many ways
for improving the business and increasing the profits
with the use of capital that I came East with the deter-
mination to form a company and carry on the business
on a proper scale to realize the largest possible profits.
Everybody is satisfied that it is the business of the
future in this country, and capital is rapidly but
blindly turning toward it. Men of experience in the
business are needed to direct it successfully. I may
here add that I have dealt in stock, more or less, all
my life, and have been in the cattle business in Colorado for the past six years. I propose to form a joint-
stock company, under the laws of either the State of
New York or Connecticut, with a capital stock of
$500,000, for the purpose of carrying on the general
business of raising, buying, fattening, and selling beef
cattle, and perhaps butchering and transporting by cars
to Eastern markets. I am now, and have been for the
past six years, part owner of the cattle and ranch of the
Huerfano Cattle Company, situated on the Huerfano
and Apache Rivers, in Huerfano and Pueblo Counties, in Southern Colorado, about thirty miles south
from Pueblo City. This ranch extends along both sides
of the above rivers for a distance of eleven miles, and
controls the adjoining Government lands as a grazing
range. The title to this ranch is held by United States
patent. The cattle now number between 5000 and
6000 head, and are American improved from Texas
cows through Kentucky bulls. Men who have seen
our stock say that we have the finest cattle in the State.
With a view to forming this stock company I have

arranged with the other owners of this ranch to turn the whole business over to the company on a low cash basis, placing cattle and land at the lowest possible figure, and the owners taking large interests in the new company.

"I have also entered into a contract with Colonel William Craig for the purchase of his extensive ranch, adjoining ours on the east, on the Huerfano and Cucharas Rivers, extending along both sides of these rivers for a distance of about seventeen miles. The title to this ranch is also secured by United States patent. The two ranches together comprise about 80,000 acres, secured by patent and platted. They embrace a river frontage of twenty-eight miles, and control a grazing range of nearly 500,000 acres, well known as one of the best grass districts of Colorado. Four thousand acres are bottom-lands under cultivation, and irrigated by ten miles of ditch. More than $150,000 worth of improvements have been put upon these ranches. Colonel George W. Schofield, major Tenth Cavalry U.S.A., formerly owner of our ranch, says, 'I have spent the last ten years in Colorado, Wyoming, New Mexico, Indian Territory, Texas, and other parts of the West, and I have never seen a more favorable location for stock-raising. It is the best cattle range I know of in all the West, and for that reason I located it.'

"It is estimated that the range will graze over 20,000 head of cattle permanently, and I propose to gradually increase the number to its full capacity. The capital stock of the company will be divided into 5000 shares of $100 each, and used as follows: For land with improvements, $325,000; for the cattle on hand at a low market value, $75,000; leaving $100,000 for a working capital with which to increase the stock and conduct the business. I propose that the company shall have an office in the East, where the books and accounts shall be kept and always open to inspection by stockholders. The treasurer of the company should be an Eastern man of undoubted character and responsibility, to whom full returns should be sent from the ranch every month or every quarter, as we now have them. I have no doubt but that the business, properly managed, on so large a scale will pay, including increased value of land and cattle, as high as fifty per cent. per annum. The profits are enormous. There is no business like it in the world, and the whole secret of it is, it costs nothing to feed the cattle. They grow without eating your money. They literally raise themselves.

"General Brisbin, writing from the Plains, says,—

"'If $200,000 were invested in Texas cattle, it would double itself in four years, and pay a semi-annual dividend of eight per cent. It should be remembered that the larger the original capital put into the business the greater would be the ratio of net profits.'

"It may be asked, 'How long will this business continue to pay such large profits? Will not capital flow into it so fast that in a few years the country will be overstocked?' The answer is plain. There is always a steady demand for beef at home, and the heavy shipments of fresh meat to other countries, amounting in the year 1877 to over ten millions of dollars in value, must constantly increase this; and there is no doubt that this country is destined to be the beef market for the whole world. No other country has such immense grass-growing districts.

" If we consult the tables, it will be observed that if cattle-breeding in the United States was stopped for five years all the cattle would be eaten up. Since 1860 four States and Territories have increased their stock, five have stood still, and thirty have decreased in comparison with the population. The rapid increase of our population will soon require that more cattle be raised, or we shall have to pay higher prices for beef. The number of people are increasing much faster than the number of cattle. The ratio of annual increase of stock in the country now is 1¾ per cent., to an annual increase of population of 2¾ per cent. So it will be seen that we must raise more cattle, or in a few years pay higher prices for beef. For ten years yet, at least, stock-growers need have no fear of overstocking the market. The beef business cannot be overdone. The census of the United States will probably show a population in 1880 of not less than 47,000,000 of people, and the cattle-raising does not keep pace with this rapid increase. In the Eastern and Middle States there has been a rapid decrease of cattle, and in a few years the West will be called on to supply almost the whole Eastern demand. Land worth over $10 per acre is too valuable to be devoted to stock-raising, and farmers can do better in cereals.

" It is for this reason that our Eastern farmers are giving up cattle-breeding and devoting their land to growing corn, wheat, rye, oats, and vegetables. They

cannot compete with Plains beef, for, while hay and
other fodder has to be cut for winter feeding there,
on the Plains the cattle run at large all winter, the
natural grasses curing on the ground, and keeping the
cattle fat nearly all winter.

" It has been the custom heretofore among cattle-men
in Colorado and elsewhere in the West to depend entirely upon grass for fattening cattle for market, and,
consequently, sales cannot always be made to advantage
unless the grass is in unusually good condition; but I
propose to grow corn, and feed sufficient to keep a certain number of steers in excellent condition for market
at any time, and have it generally known that fat cattle
can always be had at our ranch.   Corn can be raised on
the ranch as cheaply as in Kansas, thus saving the
freight and adding largely to the value of the cattle,
because of their better condition for market.

" It may be asked, ' Is it desirable to invest so much
money in land ?'   I reply that it is absolutely necessary
to own a large part of your range, especially the water-
front, so as to keep out sheep-men, settlers, and other
cattle-owners.   Sheep and cattle cannot be grazed together, and the interests should be entirely separate.
Government lands, where watering-places exist, are fast
becoming occupied by settlers and colonies, and very
soon the opportunities for locating large ranches will
entirely disappear.   In a few years at the most it will
not be possible—it is scarcely so now in Colorado—to
obtain a range where the cattle business can be conducted on a large scale.   The longer, therefore, these
large ranges are kept intact the more valuable will they

become for any purpose. It should be carefully remembered that large ranches can be managed with much greater profit than small ones.

"The ranches I now have possession of together make one of the largest, if not actually the largest, in Colorado, and are situated in the most favored portion of the State. There is hardly an advantage belonging to the country or the business which they do not possess. They have good buildings, extensive fences, bluffs and cañons for sheltering cattle in winter, and always an abundance of grass and water. There are several fine water-privileges and a large supply of pine timber close at hand. Besides the rivers spoken of, there are numerous never-failing natural springs and lakes, and many excellent opportunities for storing water in reservoirs at small cost. Among others the several species of the grama grass abound, and of its nutritious qualities I add the following, taken from the ' United States Land-Office Reports for 1869,' page 147:

" ' The most valuable and widely distributed of these (grasses) is the grama grass, its peculiar value consisting in its adaptation to all the requirements of an arid climate. It grows during the rainy season, and ripens a large quantity of seed as the dry season approaches, while the leaf and stem retain most of their nutritive qualities in drying, forming superior feed for grazing animals during the entire season.'

" Governor McCook writes of cattle-growing in Colorado:

" ' The natural grasses of our hills and valleys are equal in nutritious qualities to the Hungarian or other cultivated grasses of the East, and their abundance is such that the herds of a dozen States could have fine pasturage; and the winters are so mild that shelter or hay is unnecessary. The natural increase of cattle is 80 per cent. per annum.'

"J. W. Iliff, late the great cattle-owner of the West, wrote:

"'I have been engaged in the stock business in Colorado and Wyoming for the past fourteen years. During all that time I have grazed stock in nearly all the valleys of these Territories, both summer and winter. The cost of both summering and wintering is simply the cost of herding, as no feed nor shelter is required. I consider the summer-cured grass of these Plains and valleys as superior to any hay. My cattle have not only kept in good order on this grass through all the eight winters, but many of them, thin in the fall, have become fine beef by spring. The percentage of loss in wintering here is much less than in the States, where cattle are stabled and fed on corn and hay.'

"Mr. Iliff, at the time of his death last winter, owned 20,000 acres of water-front and was fast buying more, thus recognizing the necessity of owning his ranges. His cattle numbered over 30,000 head, and he was called the 'Colorado Cattle-king.' He began with nothing.

"I wish again to call attention to the favorable location of our ranch, on account of its ready access to railroad facilities, and thus to market. The Denver and Rio Grande Railroad just touches the western end of it, and the station is about two miles from our ranch-house. From the house to Pueblo it is about thirty miles. From the eastern end of the ranch it is eighteen miles to Pueblo, over a broad, splendid driving-road, and fourteen miles to the Arkansas River, and the Atchison, Topeka and Santa Fé Railroad along the river. This is the great through route to the East, over which most of the stock is shipped.

"The following distinguished gentlemen are familiar with this ranch and the surrounding country. They have visited it when the residence of Colonel Craig, a well-known army officer, now retired, and will, no doubt, vouch for what is here said relating to its favorable location and many great advantages: General W. T. Sherman, Major-General John Pope, Major-General John M. Schofield, Inspector-General Marcy, U. S. A.; Hon. John D. Perry, ex-President Kansas Pacific Railroad; Hon. John P. Usher, ex-Secretary Interior; Senator Chaffee, and Representative Thomas M. Patterson, of Colorado.

"General Brisbin, your correspondent, writing from the Plains in February last, seems to think that the northern country furnishes superior advantages over the southern on account of cooler climate, cattle being less liable to disease. That would be true of New Mexico, perhaps, but not of our ranch, situated as it is between the two extremes. We have not known in our six years' experience a single disease among our cattle. Our loss in winter has not, so far as we can determine, ever reached two per cent. even. It has been so small as not to be reckoned in our estimates at any time. But how is it at the north from Denver to

18

Cheyenne? Seven years ago a severe winter killed off nearly one-half of all the stock in that section of the country, and only last March, your readers will remember, there came such a blast of cold weather and such deep snows that the railroads were blocked for days and the cattle and sheep perished by thousands. At the same time our ranch was entirely free from disaster of every kind. The storm did not reach below the divide between Denver and Pueblo.

"The winter has been mild and pleasant, and no more snow has fallen than was sufficient to start the grass in the spring. Actual settlers, who have lived there for twenty years past, say that they have never known a winter severe enough to kill grazing-stock. We are two hundred and fifty miles south from Cheyenne, on the Pacific Railroad; one hundred and fifty miles south from Denver, on the Kansas Pacific Railroad; and one hundred miles south from the divide between Denver and Pueblo. South of this divide deep and lasting snows, the terror to stock, are never known. We are too far north to be subject to diseases induced by warm climates, and too far south to experience severe winters.

"I do not hesitate to say that this is the grandest opportunity for investment that can be offered. There are no uncertain risks attached to the business to eat up the profits, as the losses are almost nothing and the profits many times those afforded by other investments. As to profits, I quote your correspondent on the ground:

"'In cattle-raising in Colorado, General Cameron puts

the profits at 50 to 55 per cent. per annum on the capital invested, over and above all expenses and losses of every kind.'

" Mr. J. L. Brush, a reliable gentleman of Weld County, Colorado, says, ' I think the average profit on capital invested in cattle will not fall short of 40 per cent. per annum over and above all expenses. It is a well-known fact that stock-men in Colorado have paid from 18 to 24 per cent. interest per annum for money to invest in the cattle business, and have then made large profits.'

" We have had to learn by experience, having gone into the business without fully understanding how to conduct it in the Far West, and with only our New England farm experience to guide us. Although laboring under many disadvantages, which exist no longer, we have paid all our expenses, greatly improved our range, changed our Texas into American cattle, increased our original capital more than threefold, and realized large dividends from the business.

" I have carefully prepared the following schedule, showing the increase of a herd of 4000 cows for seven years. We would have this number by adding 2000 to our present herd. I have allowed a large margin—20 per cent.—for loss in various ways. I have found by experience that the calves average about half heifers and half steers. One of the greatest sources of profit will be in buying two-year-old steers, keeping them a year or a little longer at almost no additional expense, and selling them at an advance of $10 or more per head. This branch of the business is a great deal more profitable than raising cattle, even though that yields such enormous results. This schedule is made with reference entirely to grass-fed cattle, but fattening with corn and other feed grown on the ranch will be an additional source of large and never-failing profit.

" The first column indicates the year ; the second, the number of cows ; the third, the number of calves ; the fourth, the number of heifer calves ; the fifth, the value when yearlings, at $10 per head ; the sixth, increased value when two years old, at $5 per head ; the seventh, increased value when three years old, at $3 per head ; the eighth, the value when three years old, at $18 per head :

1st	4,000	3,200	1,600	$16,000	$8,000	$4,800	$28,800
2d	4,000	3,200	1,600	16,000	8,000	4,800	28,800
3d	5,600	4,480	2,240	22,400	11,200	6,720	40,320
4th	7,200	5,760	2,880	28,800	14,400	8,640	51,840
5th	9,440	7,552	3,776	37,760	18,880		56,640
6th	12,320	9,856	4,928	49,280			49,280
7th	16,096	12,877	6,438 at $6 per head	.	.	.	38,627
Original cows, at $18 per head		.	.	.	.	.	72,000

Total $366,308

" The first column of the next table indicates the year ; the second, the number of steer calves ; the third, the value when yearlings, at $10 per head ; the fourth, the increased value when two years old, at $6 per head ; the fifth, the increased value when three years old, at $10 per head ; the sixth, the value when three years old, at $26 per head :

1st	1,600	$16,000	$9,600	$16,000	$41,600
2d	1,600	16,000	9,600	16,000	41,600
3d	2,240	22,400	13,440	22,400	58,240
4th	2,880	28,800	17,280	28,800	74,880
5th	3,776	37,760	22,656		60,416
6th	4,928	49,280			49,280
7th	6,438 at $6 per head	.	.	. . . .	38,628

Total $364,644

Total product in seven years of 4000 cows, costing
$72,000, including cost of cows .   .   . $730,952

"The profits, or increase, on the seventh year alone would be $254,792, or 50 per cent. on the entire capital of $500,000. Each subsequent year the increase of profits is enormously enhanced.

"Each year, also, from 3000 to 5000 head of steers would be bought, and sold a year later at a profit of $10 or more per head, which item alone would pay double the expenses of the entire ranch.

"There are many plans and details connected with this enterprise which cannot well be explained in a letter of this kind without making it of great length, and which would not be thoroughly understood without reference to maps of the property and a personal interview with the author. To assure your readers that this is a perfectly legitimate enterprise, and will be organized and conducted in a practical, business-like manner, I take great pleasure in referring by special permission to the following well-known gentlemen, several of whom, with myself, will take large interests in this organization:

"General Joseph R. Hawley, late President United States Centennial Commission.

"His Excellency Governor Richard D. Hubbard, Hartford, Connecticut.

"Hon. David Clark, Hartford, Connecticut.

"Hon. Salem H. Wales, 520 Fifth Avenue, New York City.

"Hon. De Witt C. Wheeler, Police Commissioner, New York City.

"Hon. William D. Bishop, President New York, New Haven and Hartford Railroad.

"Hon. Nathaniel Wheeler, President Wheeler & Wilson Sewing-Machine Company.

"Hon. P. T. Barnum, Bridgeport, Connecticut.

"Hanford Lyon, Esq., President Bridgeport National Bank, Bridgeport, Connecticut.

"G. B. Waller, Esq., President City National Bank, Bridgeport, Connecticut.

"Samuel W. Baldwin, Esq., President Connecticut National Bank, Bridgeport, Connecticut.

"Charles B. Hotchkiss, Esq., President Pequonnock National Bank, Bridgeport, Connecticut.

"David M. Read, Esq., President of Board of Trade, Bridgeport, Connecticut.

"Nathan Seeley, Esq., of Averill Chemical Paint Company, Burling Slip, New York.

"Professor John E. Clark, Yale Scientific School, New Haven, Connecticut.

"Professor Clark thoroughly understands the country, having surveyed within ten miles of the ranch.

"The Hon. Salem H. Wales has kindly consented to

act as treasurer of the organization, and will receive subscriptions to the stock at his office, No. 10 Spruce Street, New York City.

"DAVID W. SHERWOOD."

The following letter to *Wilkes' Spirit* will be of interest to those who have read this book:

"MORE CATTLE-GROWING OUT WEST.

"DEAR SPIRIT,—Observing several articles on the cattle-project at the West lately in your paper, I therefore have simply taken some pieces from my scrapbook, and can myself vouch for their being authentic, being a pioneer of six years' standing. Stock of all kinds grazing the whole year seems marvellous to any one at the East. When they take into consideration the altitude above the sea-level (7500 feet), temperature frequently twenty degrees below zero, the whole story is in a nutshell. The grass naturally cures on the stalk and becomes hay. Of bunch-grass there are several varieties,—two named *Triticum strigosum*, Stead., the best for cattle; *Stipa spartea*, Trim., often called porcupine grass. Of all grasses which grow without cultivation in any clime on the face of the globe, we doubt if there is any which possesses as much nutriment the year round, or upon which stock fatten better than the bunch-grass of Wyoming. Clover, blue-grass, and the far-famed mezquite of Texas sink into insignificance when compared to it. This assertion will not be questioned by any one acquainted with its merits, or who has seen the fine beef or mutton in our markets from June until June again.

"There are several varieties of this grass, two of which are the most common and generally known,— one with a blade that resembles blue-grass, and stems which run up in a cluster and bear seed of much the kind that blue-grass does except that it does not form a turf, but grows in bunches, and is found in high rolling bench-land, parks, and mountains. The other kind grows more frequently upon the first bench, and may be thus described : The blade is sharp and the heads all turn to one side, and, from the broad boot on the seed-stalk, it is often called flag-grass : as to the quantity to the acre, there is little or no difference. The latter kind is usually preferred for cattle, but the former is preferred for sheep, yet either is very fine for both. These grasses start forth in the early spring and grow very rapidly ; in ordinary springs the grass is headed out by the first of June. The height of the grass is usually eighteen inches, yet, under favorable circumstances, it grows much higher. By the last of June the heads are ripe, and, in ordinary seasons, the blades are all nicely cured by the middle of July, and the whole landscape is as brown as a field of grain ready for the sickle, and would burn if set on fire. There is no time that stock takes on fat better than in the early autumn. The cured grass retains its nutriment all winter, from the fact that we have no drenching rains in the autumn to bleach it ; the light snows that come in the early winter and melt off soon only serve to moisten it and make it more palatable. When we have late summer rains and the grass remains green until frost comes (which is generally early), it is injured, and stock does not seem to do as well as when it dries up early, as is generally the case. During the winter the lowlands and sharp foot-hills are, for the most part, free from snow. Usually the snow is chased away by the winds, except that which is driven into the thick cluster of grass and becomes bedded among the old blades of other years. While grazing, stock gathers up more or less snow, which serves in a great measure as a substitute for water. When the snow departs in the spring, stock goes to the foot-hills, following up the receding snow, the grass which lies covered all winter being relished best, and, besides, the young crop starts first and grows fastest among the sharp foot-hills. In the States young grass seems to have a weakening effect upon stock, and here it comes forth among the old crop, and is so well mixed that there is scarcely any difference between the old and new. Many have claimed that it could not induce close pasturage, but experience and practical tests have proved to the contrary. It is a perennial, yet, when the root becomes killed, the seeds are so generally distributed by the winds that a barren tract will become covered.

" WHAT ONE MAN CAN DO.

" Iliff, the Cattle-king of the Plains, now deceased, had a range of one hundred and fifty miles long and a herd of cattle numbering 26,000, and was called the great Cattle-king of the Plains, and had the boss ranch in this Western country.   This ranch is in Northern Colorado ; it begins at Julesburgh, on the Union Pacific Railroad, and extends to Greeley, one hundred and fifty-six miles west ; its southern boundary is the South Platte River ; its northern, the divide, rocky and bluff, just south of the Lodge Pole Creek.   It has nearly the shape of a right-angle triangle, the right angle being at Greeley, the base-line being the South Platte River. The streams that flow from it are, first, the river just mentioned, Crow Creek, and other small creeks that take their rise in living springs in and near the bluff just mentioned and flow in a southerly direction, and empty into the South Platte River.   It includes bottom and upland range, and has several camps and ranches. The chief ranch is nearly south of Sidney, and about forty miles from Julesburgh.   At this ranch there are horses, sheds, stables, corrals, and more than two sections of land fenced.   All cattle bought by Mr. Iliff were rebranded and turned over here.   Here are the private stock-yards, corrals, sheds, pens, and all necessary conveniences for handling of cattle.   It is near the river, and of course has fine watering facilities, while from the adjoining bottom-lands plenty of hay can be cut for the use of the horses employed in herding.   No hay for cattle is cut.   They live the entire year upon the rich native grass upon the range, and, with the exception of a severe winter now and then, the percentage of loss is not very great.   Mr. Iliff was a thorough cattle-man, and from his long experience had a perfect knowledge of the business.   He began in 1860, and during the war had government contracts to fill in New

Mexico and other frontier Territories. He supplied most of the beef to the contractors who built the Union Pacific Railroad, and brought immense herds from Texas and the Indian Territory, which were driven along the line of the Union Pacific Railroad to supply the army of laborers. He had been engaged in the stock business in Kansas and New Mexico, and now in Colorado, and the present location is admirably adapted to it if the sheep-men will only keep out. Cattle and sheep do not do well together on the same range. Success in either requires separation. Mr. Iliff had purchased and owned 20,000 acres of the range when he died, which of course includes the choice springs and watering-places within its limits, and his heirs will undoubtedly purchase more when it comes into market. His herd comprised more than 26,000 head of cattle, of all ages, sizes, and conditions. The number of calves branded on his range in 1876 were 5000 head, and his sales of three- and four-year-olds amounted to nearly the same number. He realized nearly $32 per head net on the sales. At this 4000 head would bring him in the snug income of $128,000. To take care of this immense herd he employed from twelve to thirty men, very few usually in the winter months, and the largest number during the 'round-ups' in the spring. During the shipping season of 1875 he had twenty-four men, who were employed in 'cutting out' of his herd of four-year-olds the fat three-year-olds and fat cows that were no longer of any use for breeding purposes. While engaged in this work the same men gathered the cows with unbranded calves, which they put into corrals near

ne. Some mutton has also bee shipped out
tate, fourteen cases having beenhipped from
gh alone. The price of much greater
than it price

tri
lambs, $2; wethers,
shipments of sheep are not explain
come in late in the season, nd gene
ab, so that they cannot be cure before
in, thus causing them to losso their pur-
iderable quantities of wool; lnce the first
good, though after that tin they shear

by, and after the calves were branded they were turned out on the range again.

"The wool-shipments from the West for 1873 in Wyoming alone were 85,077 pounds; for 1874, 215,-242 pounds; 1875, 228,033 pounds; 1876, 333,919 pounds; 1877, 346,280 pounds; 1878, 400,000 pounds. The cattle-cars carry twenty head per car, and there was shipped last year by Iliff & Co. 32,480. These cattle yielded a net income to their owners of $30 per head, making an aggregate sum of $974,000. The cattle literally raised themselves; they had been on the range from one year to another, without shelter or hay.

" Winter grazing in Wyoming has become an established fact. I have already taken up so much of your valuable space I am afraid I shall be barred out, but, in conclusion, I would like to add I am doing something in the stock business,—ship annually to Boston tons of wool and round up hundreds of cows and horses. I will also add I am very enthusiastic about stock-growing associations. But if I get started on this, there is no one on the range can stop me, so I will close at once.   W. J. O."

I cannot give a more fitting close to a book like this than by making the following quotation concerning the wool-clip of Colorado during the past year:

In 1879, 2,000,000 head of sheep were sheared in Colorado, the average weight of fleece being three and a half pounds, and the average price paid 20 cents per pound, the amount realized reaching $1,400,000 on wool alone. Some mutton has also been shipped out of the State, fourteen cases having been shipped from Julesburgh alone. The price of wool was much greater last year than it was in 1878, and the advance in price has been regular and still continues. Wool which brought 22 cents in Colorado last spring is now selling for 35 cents in Boston, and would, if to be had, be worth 31 cents here now. Mr. Wright estimates that 500,000 lambs were added to the number of sheep in the State during the year. Several thousand head of sheep were also driven in from outside points,—California contributing 45,000, which were sold, upon arrival, at: lambs, $2; wethers, $2.50; ewes, $3. The California shipments of sheep are not especially popular. They come in late in the season, and generally with the scab, so that they cannot be cured before cold weather sets in, thus causing them to lose to their purchasers considerable quantities of wool; hence the first clip is not so good, though after that time they shear more heavily than Colorado breeds.

INDEX.

THE END.

MRS. FORRESTER'S NOVELS.

12mo. Extra cloth. $1.25 each. 16mo. Paper
cover. 50 cts. each.

RHONA.

" The author is one of the most popular writers of the period, and this is esteemed among her best."— *Baltimore Gazette.*

DOLORES.

" This is a delightful book. One of the best romances of the day."—*Philadelphia Chronicle.*

DIANA CAREW;

Or, For a Woman's Sake.

" A story of great beauty and complete interest to its close."—*Boston Traveller.*

MIGNON.

" Will be counted her best, as it is full of a keen interest both in its plot and character, and is written in a refined and exceedingly pleasing style."—*Publishers' Weekly.*

VIVA.

" A work of unusual power and interest. The plot is deeply attractive, the characters are striking, and the management of the story throughout is very skilful."—*Boston Saturday Evening Gazette.*

THE " DUCHESS " SERIES.

PHYLLIS.

12mo. Extra cloth. $1.25. 16mo. Paper cover. 50 cts.

" It is fascinating to a high degree. . . . We lay aside the book with a sigh of regret that the pleasure is over, after mingling our laughter and tears with the varying fortunes of the charming heroine."—*New York Ev. Mail.*

" Certainly ' Phyllis' is one of the most fascinating little novels that has appeared this year."—*N. O. Times.*

MOLLY BAWN.

12mo. Extra cloth. $1.25. 16mo. Paper cover. 60 cts.

" Is really an attractive novel. Full of wit, spirit, and gayety, the book contains, nevertheless, touches of the most exquisite pathos. There is plenty of fun and humor, which never degenerate into vulgarity. All women will envy, and all men fall in love with, her. Higher praise we surely cannot give."—*London Athenæum.*

AIRY FAIRY LILIAN.

12mo. Extra cloth. $1.25. 16mo. Paper cover. 60 cts.

" The airiest and most sparkling contribution of the month is a brilliant romance by the author of ' Phyllis.' It is as full of variety and refreshment as a bright and changeful June morning. Its narrative is animated, its dialogue crisp and spirited, its tone pure and wholesome, and its characters are gracefully contrasted."—*Harper's Magazine.*

J. B. LIPPINCOTT & CO.'S DICTIONARIES
OF THE
French, German, and Spanish Languages.

CONTANSEAU'S PRACTICAL DICTIONARY OF THE FRENCH and English Languages. Composed from the French dictionaries of the Academy, Boiste, Bescherelle, etc , and from the best English dictionaries, followed by abridged Vocabularies of geographical and mythological names By LEON CONTANSEAU Crown 8vo. Extra cloth. $2.50.

CONTANSEAU'S POCKET DICTIONARY OF THE FRENCH and English Languages. By LEON CONTANSEAU. 18mo. Extra cloth $1.50. *Tourist's Edition*. 2 Volumes. 32mo. Cloth flexible. In case. $1.75

LONGMAN'S POCKET DICTIONARY OF THE GERMAN AND English Languages. By F. W. LONGMAN, Balliol College, Oxford. 18mo. Extra cloth. $1 50. *Tourist's Edition*. 2 Volumes. 32mo. Cloth flexible. In case. $1.75.

"We have not seen any pocket dictionary (German and English) that can bear comparison with this. It is remarkably compendious, and the arrangement is clear."—*London Athenæum.*

NEUMAN AND BARETTI'S POCKET DICTIONARY OF THE Spanish and English Languages. Compiled from the last improved edition. 18mo. Extra cloth. $1.50.

ANNOTATED POEMS OF ENGLISH AUTHORS.
EDITED BY THE
Rev. EDWARD T. STEVENS, M.A. Oxford,
and Rev. DAVID MORRIS, B.A. London.

16mo. With Illustrations. Bound in cloth, limp.

THIS SERIES INCLUDES:

GRAY'S ELEGY IN A COUNTRY CHURCH-YARD. Price, 20 cents.

COWPER'S TASK. Book I. THE SOFA. Price, 25 cents.

GOLDSMITH'S DESERTED VILLAGE. Price, 20 cents.

SCOTT'S LADY OF THE LAKE. Canto I. Price, 35 cents.

GOLDSMITH'S TRAVELLER. Price, 25 cents.

The above Series bound in ONE VOLUME. *Illustrated. 16mo. Extra cloth.* $1.00.

"It is a good work well done, and we cannot commend the little Volume too earnestly to the attention of teachers who are wise enough to appreciate the need there is for giving a larger and better place to English classic literature than it now has in our schemes of education."—*New York Evening Post*

"The growing interest manifested in all our American schools in the study of the English classics will make these little Volumes eminently useful."—*New England Journ. of Education*

STANDARD
Architectural Works.

SLOAN'S HOMESTEAD ARCHITECTURE.

Containing Forty Designs for Villas, Cottages, and Farm Houses,
with Essays on Style, Construction, Landscape
Gardening, Furniture, etc.

Illustrated with over 100 Engravings. By Samuel Sloan, Architect.
Second Edition. 8vo. Extra cloth. $3.50.

HOBBS'S RURAL ARCHITECTURE.

Containing Designs and Ground Plans for Villas and other Edifices,
both Suburban and Rural, Adapted to the United States.

With Rules for Criticism, and an Introduction. By Isaac H. Hobbs & Son,
Architects Illustrated with over 100 Engravings. 8vo. Extra cloth. $3.00.

SLOAN'S CONSTRUCTIVE ARCHITECTURE.

A Guide to the Practical Builder and Mechanic.

In which is contained a Series of Designs for Domes, Roofs, Spires, the
Interior Construction and Finish of Bays, Window Shutters, Sliding Doors,
etc. Illustrated by 66 Plates. With Explanatory Text. By Samuel Sloan,
Architect. Quarto. Cloth. $7 50.

CITY AND SUBURBAN ARCHITECTURE.

Containing Numerous Designs and Details for Public Edifices,
Private Residences, and Mercantile Buildings.

Illustrated with 131 Plates. With Explanatory Text. By Samuel Sloan,
Architect. Folio. Extra cloth. $10.00.

THE MODEL ARCHITECT.

A Series of Original Designs for Cottages, Villas, Suburban
Residences, etc.

Accompanied by Explanations, Specifications, Estimates, and Elaborate
Details. With 210 Plates, the majority of which are handsomely colored. By
Samuel Sloan, Architect. Two Volumes. Imperial quarto. Half Turkey.
$18.00.

THE

"ODD TRUMP" SERIES.

8vo. Fine cloth. $1.25. Paper cover. 75 cts.

THE ODD TRUMP.

" Deserving the highest praise. . . . Its incidents are all pure; it is the apotheosis of chivalric bravery and courtesy; and is written in elegant English, with a purity of style that is in itself refreshing."—*Louisville Courier-Journal.*

HARWOOD.

" A good novel in the best sense of the word."—*Indianapolis Journal.*

THE LACY DIAMONDS.

" Will more than ever stamp its author as one of the foremost popular novelists of America, or it may be of the world."—*New York Commercial.*

FLESH AND SPIRIT.

" We do not at all wonder that these novels are popular. They deserve popularity for being precisely what they are meant to be and what they profess to be."—*New York Evening Post.*

THE CLIFTON PICTURE.

" A novel that the most exciting taste will revel in. It is brimful of situations, bright and entertaining "—*Boston Post.*

THE GHOST OF REDBROOK.

" It is a thoroughly readable novel, pure and vigorous in tone, with plenty of love, romance, and humor, and not much ghost. The plot is worked out most skilfully, and will puzzle even the inveterate novel readers."—*Louisville Courier-Journal.*

Lightning Source UK Ltd.
Milton Keynes UK
UKOW05f0604200417

299527UK00016B/378/P